AT THE TABLE OF
LA FORTEZZA

AT THE TABLE OF
LA FORTEZZA

The Enchantment of Tuscan Cooking
from the Lunigiana Region

ANNETTE JOSEPH

photography by DAVID LOFTUS

RIZZOLI
NEW YORK

New York Paris London Milan

First published in the United States of America in 2022 by
Rizzoli International Publications, Inc.
300 Park Avenue South
New York, NY 10010
www.rizzoliusa.com

Copyright © 2022 Annette Joseph
Photography by David Loftus
Additional photography: page 9, Infraordinario; page 208, Andrea Rinaldi

Publisher: Charles Miers
Editor: Gloria Nantz
Design: Janice Shay / Pinafore Press
Production Manager: Maria Pia Gramaglia
Managing Editor: Lynn Scrabis
Prop Stylist / Production: Barbara Pederzini
Food Stylist: Rosie Scott
Assistant Food Stylist: Leonardo Ceri

Printed in Singapore

2022 2023 2024 2025 / 10 9 8 7 6 5 4 3 2 1

ISBN: 978-0-8478-6948-0
Library of Congress Control Number: 2022932606

Visit us online:
Facebook.com/RizzoliNewYork
Twitter: @Rizzoli_Books
Instagram.com/RizzoliBooks
Pinterest.com/RizzoliBooks
Youtube.com/user/RizzoliNY
Issuu.com/Rizzoli

This book is dedicated to all
the slow food purveyors, food artisans,
restaurant owners, family-owned businesses,
and farmers who have taught me what it
means to eat local. This book
is a reality because of you.

TABLE OF CONTENTS

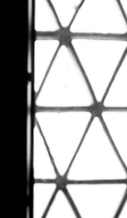

INTRODUCTION

When my husband and I bought a medieval fortress, La Fortezza, in the far northwestern region of Tuscany a few years ago, it was the rugged beauty of Lunigiana that first caught my eye. Flanked by the Liguria coastline and the Apuan Alps, this region is very different from the rolling green hills that Tuscany brings to mind. It is blanketed by rugged farmland—big and green and filled to bursting with olive groves, chestnut forests, and vineyards. This topography has given the region amazing foods and some of the best wines and olives oils in all of Italy.

Lunigiana is wedged between two culinary giants: Liguria, on the northwestern coastline of Italy, is known for its seafood, focaccia, and pesto; and Emilia-Romagna, called the breadbasket of Italy, produces pork, prosciutto, Parmesan cheese, balsamic vinegar, and fantastic beef. The Lunigiana region brings together the delicate textures and unique flavors of both the coast and the mountains, and all of these simple delicacies make for delicious results in the kitchen. The tasty meat of the Zeri lamb, the local chestnut honey that pairs well with our sheep and goat cheeses, and the ancient chestnut-flour-based bread (*marocca*) and pastas are a few key ingredients of tasty rustic food at its best. This region is also known for its traditional and ancient medieval methods, including cooking over an open fire.

Some of the recipes featured in this book date back to the Middle Ages. The preservation of traditional cooking methods is one of the reasons this area is recognized by UNESCO as a Biosphere Reserve. As I came to know and appreciate the food here, I began to research traditional recipes, and happily spent the last several years tasting, testing, and adapting them for this cookbook, to share with you.

With the globalization of our tastes, I'm delighted to offer many dishes that Italians have loved for centuries. Because the food is seasonal, the recipes in this book are divided into four parts that serve to show what we hunt, forage, harvest, and cook throughout the year.

Everything that I cook with is part of Italy's slow food culture, and the reason I now know to cook with the finest ingredients, whether you're making a holiday meal or just toast and jam.

With the exception of Modena, where our balsamic vinegar comes from, and Parma, where our Parmesan cheese is produced, everything is sourced not more than thirty miles from La Fortezza. Most vegetables, fruit, and herbs come directly from our own kitchen garden. We are lucky to have wine from our vineyard, and mushrooms from the nearby forest. Animals are hunted in the area, and butchered down the road. The dairy provides us with all of our milk products. I buy regularly and seasonally from local shepherds, fishermen, beekeepers, olive presses, flour mills, and truffle hunters. This is key to the simple, delicious food that's part of the fabric of Italian country life—and, I am happy to say, it hasn't changed for hundreds of years.

So, I urge you to find the best ingredients that are available to you, not only when you prepare these recipes, but for each dish you cook. Plant a garden and eat what you've grown. In the back of this book I have provided a resource list to help you find the best products that may not be available locally. Here, I like to say that we eat a "zero-kilometer diet," which means everything we eat is right in our backyard. It's a great rule to live by, and to live longer.

Part 1: Spring / *Primavera*

Spring in the region known as Lunigiana is always unpredictable. May brings torrential downpours, the land swells, and rivers run wild. The temperatures range from cold to tepid to hot. The kitchen garden needs to be planted at the perfect time—this usually means the first week of June at La Fortezza. We start summer planting with tomatoes, herbs, fennel, and zucchini, peppers, and eggplant. The strawberries begin to appear and delicate basil plants take root. In the spring, artichokes and bitter greens, along with the onions and carrots, are ready to be harvested from our garden.

The orchard's blossoms are bursting despite the weather conditions. They wait patiently for the sun to regularly appear. In the kitchen I utilize all the greens I can get my hands on. I love to prepare artichokes in all sorts of variations. Fava beans show up on the menu, and we ready ourselves for the first harvest of zucchini flowers, which seem to pop up within a few weeks of planting. The first whispers of feathery fennel appear in the herb garden, their tender shoots perfect for salads and on fish.

I take care to ration the last of the previous year's chestnut flour. It is carefully measured so we have a supply until the next milling in the fall. Young lamb, fresh fish, and porcini mushrooms are delivered to the kitchen door. The open-air markets are in full swing by mid-June. Bottles of wine from our vineyard are delivered in cases, in anticipation of aperitivi on the terrace throughout the summer. Once the rain disappears we begin dining on the terrace. Spring is the beginning of all life on the grounds of La Fortezza, a time for planting and planning as I sit under our cherry tree and dream of what's to come.

Part 2: Summer / *Estate*

Summer is the season of village *sagre* (local food festivals), and each nearby village has its own specialty. We love going in the evening, and sampling all the regional foods made by our friends and neighbors, like *sgabei* (fried dough) and *panigacci* (what I like to call an Italian taco). There are lots of live bands and dancing and, of course, eating.

Our kitchen garden also becomes fulsome and festive. The summer heat kicks in and tomatoes start to ripen and sweeten in the hot sun. Each week I make fresh *passata*, crushed fresh tomatoes that I use in so many recipes, including our own tomato sauce, and on pasta and pizza. The local forager delivers tons of delicate, bright electric-yellow galletti mushrooms that I use to top crostini. The basil is abundant and spills over the beds, begging to be watered. Most days we dine on salads with tomatoes from our garden warmed by the sun and paired with fresh focaccia, served with homemade pesto and melt-in-your-mouth burrata. As the sun begins to set, we head to aperitivo on the terrace, which regularly consists of charred eggplant, doused with the local olive oil, then sopped up with leftover focaccia from lunch, along with salty olives. I grill daily, and almost all of the vegetables from the garden are grilled, especially the peppers. I pickle summer vegetables to enjoy beyond summer, and make a savory tart with greens that is a local specialty. I use every inch of the garden and all the fresh herbs—nothing goes to waste. The summer bounty is a gift that I try to save and experience in dishes throughout the year.

Part 3: Autumn / *Autunno*

In my opinion, autumn is the champion season in our region. It is the time when the most important harvests take place—the harvests of grapes and olives. When I see our vintner's trucks rumbling down the hill—one full of people, dogs, and picnic

baskets and another packed to the brim with colorful empty grape bins—I know it's going to be a great week. Our vineyard is run by a family that has harvested on our property for many years—too many to remember, as they claim. I use our red wine in the boar stew recipe, and the white in risotto. We use all the grapes we can get our hands on for making our friend Giovanna's recipe for grape jelly, and I top off focaccia with roasted grapes.

Once the grapes are picked and off to be fermented into wine, we can focus on the next event, which is the olive harvest. I watch the olives mature over the summer, and usually by the end of September into November we are ready to harvest. The olive harvest is deeply romanticized. I remember when I was invited to my first-ever olive harvest, I was so excited—no one told me what hard work it was! Not only were there virtually millions of olives to be picked, but they needed to be handled with care so as not to bruise them. I went home at the end of the day stiff and exhausted. But now I have a huge appreciation for fresh olive oil and what it takes to produce just one bottle. In October everyone from the community goes to the olive press (*il frantoio*) to wait for their oil to be pressed and to be weighed. The yield varies every year, and waiting to see if you had a good year is very emotional for Italians.

Our kitchen garden yields pumpkins and gourds. We start seeing more porcini mushrooms. I smoke pumpkins in the *forno*, or over an open fire, tossed into the ashes; slow-smoked pumpkin with toasted hazelnuts and pecorino is one of my favorite dishes. The smoky flavor adds to the natural sweetness of the pumpkin, and the addition of crunchy toasted hazelnuts and sharp pecorino cheese is incredible. This is also the time for truffles. I forage with our friend Simone the truffle hunter and his amazing truffle dog, Tito, and shave truffles on almost anything I cook.

The autumn season brings bold flavors to the kitchen, and we savor every taste and scent. The crisp air begins to roll in and in the olive groves branches are trimmed and burned. The smoke hangs in the air. October brings the sharp taste of the first-press olive oil. It is something I look forward to every year.

Part 4: Winter / *Inverno*

By mid-November there are signs that winter is upon us. We use our forno for the very last time before the winds begin to whip and the bone-chilling cold drives us indoors to light the fireplaces. I make pizza using our homemade jarred tomato sauce and preserved vegetables. In late October, the hunters deliver meat in exchange for our letting them hunt on the property. I make boar stew with polenta, bake rabbit with apples, and cook other hearty and comforting dishes. I add our stash of truffles to rich pastas. The last of the tomatoes go into a warm kale salad along with chickpeas. Soups, like chickpea soup with pancetta, are a staple when the first snow appears on the mountaintops.

This is the season that chestnut flour is milled, so I make chestnut bread, chestnut gnocchi with bitter greens, chocolate chestnut-flour Bundt cake, and chestnut fritters for dessert, with ricotta and chestnut honey. The holidays in Italy are the time to make the rounds of beautiful little Christmas markets that pop up all over. I like to pick up jarred delicacies like the local truffle honey and Christmas cakes to add to our larder and serve to guests, and to give as gifts.

The snow on the mountains is picture-perfect beautiful and pulls me outside, away from our warm kitchen and fireplaces, to enjoy the season. I feel a deep connection to the land throughout the year, and I experience the seasons much more fully now, through the food and the recipes I offer in this book.

Mangiamo!

SPRING
RECIPES

....

ARTICHOKES *with Anchovies*
(CARCIOFI CON L'ACCIUGATA)

Stuffed artichokes were new to me. I first tasted them at a "workers' lunch" with friends—water, wine, primo, secondo, and a coffee, for a set price of around 10 euros. The workers' lunch is an institution in Italy and a wonderful experience throughout the EU. These artichokes were delicious, so I asked my girlfriends for a recipe. You should know that Italians always leave an ingredient or two out of recipes—when I ask if that's because they forgot or if it was on purpose, they usually admit to both. In this recipe, I've added what I thought was missing. ✄ *Serves 8*

For the artichokes:

2 lemons, halved

8 small to medium artichokes

¼ cup extra virgin olive oil

1 teaspoon salt

¼ teaspoon freshly ground black pepper

For the stuffing:

3 tablespoons extra virgin olive oil, plus more for drizzling

6 flat anchovy fillets packed in oil, drained

2 tablespoons fresh lemon juice (about ½ lemon)

1 cup coarse fresh breadcrumbs (from day-old focaccia or a crusty bread)

½ teaspoon salt

½ teaspoon freshly ground black pepper

½ cup grated Parmesan cheese

2 tablespoons chopped fresh flat-leaf parsley

To prepare the artichokes: Pour 2 cups water into a large bowl then squeeze the lemon juice into the water and toss in the spent lemon halves as well.

Using a serrated knife, remove the top 1 inch of an artichoke and bend back the outer leaves until they snap off close to base. Keep peeling until you reach the tender center leaves. With a paring knife, peel the stem down to its pale inner core. Place the cleaned artichoke into the lemon water. Repeat the process for the remaining artichokes.

In a large pot with a lid, pour 4 cups water and the oil, and bring to a simmer over medium heat. Place the artichokes and the lemon halves into the pot, and season with salt and pepper. Cover and reduce the heat to medium-low, and simmer for 20 to 30 minutes until just tender. Transfer the artichokes to a dish to cool, and reserve the cooking liquid. When the artichokes have cooled, cut them in half lengthwise. Scoop out and discard the fuzzy center and any sharp leaves.

Note: If you want to prepare these 1 day ahead, the artichokes can be braised as described above,

then refrigerated in their cooking liquid. When you're ready to cook, remove the artichokes from the cooking liquid, reserving the liquid. Pat the artichokes dry, and bring them to room temperature before continuing with the next step.

To prepare the stuffing: Preheat the oven to 400°F.

Heat 3 tablespoons oil in a 12-inch heavy skillet over medium-high heat, then add the anchovies, mashing them into the oil with a wooden spoon. Add the artichokes and gently stir until coated. Note: You may need to do this in two batches if using larger artichokes.

Transfer the artichokes to a baking dish and drizzle with ½ cup of the reserved braising liquid mixed with the lemon juice. Sprinkle the breadcrumbs over the artichokes, and add the salt, pepper, and Parmesan. Bake for 8 to 10 minutes, or until the topping is golden brown. Sprinkle with fresh parsley, drizzle with oil, and serve warm.

FRIED ZUCCHINI FLOWERS
with Yeasted Batter
(I FIORI DI ZUCCA IN PASTELLA)

When I first planted my kitchen garden at La Fortezza, the gardener convinced me to plant four zucchini plants, but a local friend told me that was way too many, and she was right. The yield was so huge that I found myself cooking them every day for the entire season! The garden looked like a field of yellow flowers—it was a zucchini nightmare, really, because I couldn't give them away since everyone grew them. But the extra plantings yielded me tons of blossoms, and I must admit we enjoyed this recipe endlessly. These flowers are as delicate as tissue paper, so one of the first things to remember is not to wash them. If they are fresh from your garden, just brush the dirt off.
Note: The sparkling water used to activate the yeast gives the batter a lighter consistency, which is perfect for these delicate flowers. ✂ ***Serves 8***

2 cups sparkling water, at room temperature,
divided

1 tablespoon crumbled brick yeast, or substitute

1 envelope (2 ¼ teaspoons) active dry yeast

1 cup 00 flour, available in most groceries

½ teaspoon sugar

½ teaspoon salt

3 to 4 cups extra virgin olive oil, for frying

16 zucchini blossoms

1 teaspoon Maldon flake salt to finish

In a bowl, whisk together 1 cup sparkling water and the yeast, and set aside for 10 minutes or until bubbles form.

Add the flour to another bowl, and whisk in the remaining 1 cup sparkling water until well combined.

Whisk the yeast mixture into the flour mixture until just combined, then whisk in the sugar and salt. Once well mixed, cover the bowl with plastic wrap and set aside for about 30 minutes at room temperature. You will notice that the batter will have a slight foamy appearance—that is good.

Heat about 1 inch of oil in a frying pan or cast-iron skillet over medium-high heat until it reaches 325°F on a deep-fry thermometer.

When at temperature, use tongs to dip the flowers into the batter, being careful not to over batter, and place them into the hot oil. Fry three at a time for 2 to 3 minutes, then turn, using the tongs, and continue to fry another 2 minutes, until they are golden brown. Fry the remaining blossoms, adding oil as needed after each bunch.

Transfer the fried blossoms to a baking sheet lined with paper towels to drain and sprinkle with flake salt to finish. Serve immediately.

BORLOTTI BEANS AND LARDO
(FAGIOLI IN SALSA CON LARDO DI COLONNATA)

I find borlotti beans (also called cranberry beans) fresh in the market here in Fivizzano; they can be found dry as well, so don't worry about finding these at your grocery. Tuscans are bean eaters, and the love of legumes also runs true of the Lunigiana people (remember, Lunigiana is in Tuscany). Lardo is frequently used in place of olive oil as an ingredient in bean dishes to add fat, which makes everything taste good. ✂ *Serves 4*

2 cups dried borlotti beans, or 2 pounds fresh borlotti beans in the pod

½ teaspoon salt

4 ounces lardo, cut into cubes, or you may substitute pancetta

1 small onion, diced

1 pound Italian sausages (4 to 6 links), your choice of sweet or spicy

1 cup red wine

1 (14-ounce) can Mutti Polpa chopped tomatoes, or another good-quality brand

1 teaspoon dried rosemary

½ teaspoon freshly ground black pepper

Soak the dried borlotti beans for 8 hours, or overnight. Drain the beans, rinse them, and add them to a large pot; cover with cold water and bring to a boil over high heat. Once it reaches a rolling boil, reduce the heat to low and simmer for about 50 to 60 minutes; season with the salt at the end of cooking. (If using fresh beans, shell them and cook them, but there is no need to soak and they may be tender in a shorter amount of time.)

In a large Dutch oven, cook the lardo and onion over medium heat for 3 to 5 minutes, until the onion is translucent. Add the whole sausages and brown for 3 to 4 minutes. Add the wine, tomatoes, rosemary, black pepper, and the cooked beans. Reduce the heat to low and simmer for 35 to 40 minutes to combine the flavors. Serve warm in bowls with crunchy bread.

ARTICHOKE, RED PEPPER, AND TUNA SALAD

Behind the fortress, we have an artichoke grove that we harvest in early spring. I use everything that we grow. I have always been inspired by the multiple ways Italians prepare artichokes—adding them to salads, baking or frying them, or simply steaming them with butter. In this recipe, their delicate flavor balances the vinegary, tuna-stuffed peppers beautifully. This recipe works well as a lunch salad or an aperitivo snack. Unlike with larger artichokes, there is no need to open and scoop out the fibers in the baby version because they are not yet developed.

Serves 4 to 6

1 tablespoon salt

1 lemon, halved

1 pound purple or green baby artichokes (about 8 to 10)

10 ounces tuna-stuffed red peppers jarred in olive oil (see Source Guide, page 205), cut in half

½ cup finely chopped celery (from about 1 ½ stalks), including the leaves

¼ cup fresh mint leaves

¼ cup fresh basil leaves

2 tablespoons extra virgin olive oil

2 tablespoons good-quality balsamic vinegar

Fill a large pot one-third full of cool water and add the salt. Squeeze the lemon juice into the water and toss the spent lemon halves in as well.

Working with one baby artichoke at a time, pull off and discard the tough outer leaves. Rip the leaves downward toward the stem and away, so that you bring as many extra tough fibers with the leaf as possible. Keep removing the outer leaves until the remaining leaves are soft and a light green color, almost yellow. It is better to overdo it and remove a few tender leaves than to end up with tough, inedible baby artichokes.

Cut off and discard the dark and medium green tops of the remaining leaves. You can gather them on the cutting board and cut the tops off all at once. Cut off and discard the stem ends.

As you peel them, place the artichokes into the pot of lemon water so they will stay nice and green.

Simmer the artichokes over medium heat for 10 to 15 minutes until they are tender. Use a slotted spoon to remove the artichokes from the pot and set aside to cool.

Combine the tuna-stuffed peppers, celery, mint, and basil in a large serving bowl.

When the artichokes are cool, cut them in half, or quarters, depending on their size—the pieces should match the size of the tuna-stuffed peppers—and add them to the bowl.

Toss everything gently with the olive oil and balsamic vinegar. Serve at room temperature or chilled.

FARRO SALAD
with Green Beans and Pesto
(INSALATA DI FARRO CON PESTO E FAGIOLINI)

Farro is a grain grown in the Garfagnano area, near where we live. It has the look and texture of wild rice, but with a wheat-like taste. I like to use it in place of quinoa or couscous. Italians put it in soups to thicken and give them body, such as in Chickpea Soup (recipe, page 158). It's easily found in grocery stores all over America.

Serves 4

3 cups farro

1 ½ cups green beans

For the pesto:

Makes 6 to 8 cups

4 cups loosely packed fresh basil leaves, plus more for garnish

½ cup pine nuts, untoasted

½ cup grated Parmesan cheese

2 cloves garlic (optional)

1 teaspoon salt

¾ cup extra virgin olive oil

In a stockpot, bring 8 cups water to a boil over high heat. Stir in the farro, reduce the heat to low, and simmer for 40 minutes, stirring occasionally. Drain and rinse the cooked farro in cool water and set aside.

Add the green beans to a pot of boiling water and blanch them for 5 minutes, then drain the beans and plunge them into a bowl of ice water. Set aside while you make the pesto.

To make the pesto, combine 4 cups basil, the pine nuts, cheese, garlic (if using), and salt in the bowl of a food processor fitted with the metal blade. Pulse until a paste forms, stopping often to scrape down the sides. Be careful not to overprocess, as the heat tends to cook the basil and brown the leaves.

Pour the oil into the mixture and blend until smooth.

This can be made 1 day ahead and refrigerated in a lidded container. Stored in a sealed jar, it can last 2 weeks in the refrigerator.

Place the cooled farro and beans in a large bowl, toss them with 3 heaping tablespoons of pesto, garnish with basil leaves, and serve at room temperature.

RISOTTO
with Romano Beans and Peas

Romano beans are Italian flat beans, in the family of string beans, and similar to an oversized snap pea with a sweet, subtle flavor. These beans are prepared all over Italy and are a staple in Lunigiana in the spring at most farmers' markets. If you can't find them at your local market, you may substitute yellow wax beans or green beans in this recipe. If you're a home gardener, you can find Romano bean seeds online (see Source Guide, page 205) and plant your own. The addition of Romano beans adds to the sweetness of the dish and gives the risotto a richer, heartier flavor than simply adding peas alone. ✂ *Serves 6*

....

4 cups vegetable stock

2 cups shelled peas

1 cup fresh Romano beans

2 tablespoons extra virgin olive oil

3 tablespoons unsalted butter, divided

2 medium shallots, chopped

1 ½ cups Arborio rice

½ teaspoon salt

1 cup grated Parmesan cheese

¼ teaspoon freshly ground black pepper

Grated zest of 1 lemon

2 teaspoons fresh thyme leaves

....

Bring the vegetable stock to a simmer in a large saucepan over medium heat. Reduce the heat to low, and cover to keep warm.

In a stockpot over medium-high heat, bring 8 cups water to a boil; then add the peas and blanch them for 2 minutes until bright green. Remove with a large slotted spoon, and plunge the peas into a bowl of ice water. Next, add the Romano beans to the boiling water, and blanch for 2 minutes; then remove with a slotted spoon and add them to the peas in the bowl of ice water.

Once cooled, use the slotted spoon to transfer the peas and beans to a dry bowl, and set aside.

In a large sauté pan over medium heat, combine the olive oil and 1 tablespoon butter. Add the shallots, rice, and salt and stir continuously for 4 minutes, or until the rice is well coated and begins to sizzle. Add the warm stock ½ cup at a time, stirring until all the liquid is absorbed before adding more, for 18 to 20 minutes, or until the rice is al dente and the risotto becomes creamy. Then add the peas and Romano beans, cheese, the remaining 2 tablespoons butter, and the pepper, and continue to stir until the cheese and butter are melted.

Remove from the heat, garnish with the lemon zest and thyme leaves, then cover and let sit for 2 minutes. Stir before you serve.

BASIC EGG PASTA DOUGH

This is our basic pasta dough recipe; I use it consistently in all of our pasta recipes. Here at La Fortezza, rolling out pasta by hand takes about 10 to 15 minutes and is a great workout, plus it's meditative and very satisfying. You can, of course, use a machine; this recipe shares both techniques. ✄ **Makes dough for 4 servings of pasta**

1 ½ cups all-purpose flour, or you may substitute 00 flour, plus more for dusting

½ teaspoon salt

2 large eggs, plus 4 egg yolks

Semolina or corn flour, for tossing

Sift the flour and salt into a large mixing bowl. Make a well in the middle of the flour, add the eggs, and whisk them into the flour with a fork, gradually incorporating the walls of the flour into the well to form the dough. Turn it out onto a lightly floured work surface and knead the dough for 5 to 10 minutes, until it is smooth. Wrap the dough in plastic wrap, and refrigerate at least 30 minutes, or up to 4 hours, before rolling out—any longer and you risk the dough oxidizing and turning a dark color.

With a Pasta Machine: Set the pasta machine rollers on their widest setting. Cut the pasta dough into quarters. Lightly dust one quarter with flour and press it into a rectangle that's almost the width of the rollers, about 5 inches wide. You'll want to maintain this width as you roll by trimming the edges with a knife. Cover the remaining three pieces with plastic to keep from drying out.

First, feed the dough through the machine, and fold the dough in half. Repeat twice.

Then adjust the machine, set the rollers one notch thinner each time you roll the dough through until you are rolling the pasta dough on the thinnest setting. Trim the two ends with a knife so that they are straight, and put on a lightly floured surface. Now your dough is ready to shape into many types of pasta.

One tip: When you are rolling out your dough, try to use as little excess flour as possible as the flour will dry out your dough.

Rolling Pasta by Hand: Dust a wooden board or work surface with 1 tablespoon flour. Unwrap the chilled dough from the plastic wrap and flatten it with a rolling pin. Roll out the dough into a thin round sheet, less than 1/8 inch thick—you should be able to hold the sheet up to light and see the light through it.

Note: To make tagliatelle or pappardelle, cut the pasta sheet into 5-inch-wide strips, then roll each strip like a jelly roll into a 3 by 5-inch-long log. Trim the ends of the roll to make them straight. Cut into strips, depending on what type of pasta you're forming, starting on the right side of the log. Then toss the circles of pasta nests into semolina or corn flour, unfurling them into pasta nests. Continue down the log until you have 5 or 6 nests.

Notes on Cooking Pasta

I have learned to throw two handfuls of salt, about ¼ cup, into a large pot of pasta to make the water "taste like the sea," according to Italians. Don't be afraid, the pasta doesn't take on all of the salt flavor, it just makes it cook better for some reason. Pull the pasta from the pot with a spider strainer rather than pouring it into a colander because the starch content will coagulate if it sits for a few minutes and cause the pasta to stick together. Also, never rinse the pasta, because it removes the starch. Put the pasta directly into the warm pan or bowl of sauce and toss.

The starch needs to stay on the pasta so that the sauce clings to it and the flavor is absorbed.

HOMEMADE TAGLIATELLE
with Fresh Fava Beans and Potatoes Tossed in Pesto
(TAGLIATELLE CON FAVE E PATATE IN PESTO)

This recipe can be a main dish; it is so hearty and comforting. Pesto is from Liguria, not Lunigiana, but the two regions are so close that this is one of the shared aspects of their cuisines. Italians like to take all the best tastes from all the best regions, whenever possible. Fava beans (also called broad beans and pigeon beans) are high in tyramine, and shouldn't be eaten by people who take MAO inhibitors (e.g., antidepressants.) You can substitute green beans.

Serves 4

Basic Egg Pasta Dough (recipe, page 30)

3 heaping tablespoons pesto (recipe, page 27)

2 cups fresh fava beans (2 pounds of pods), cleaned

½ teaspoon salt, plus ¼ cup for cooking the pasta

1 pound Yukon Gold potatoes, peeled and cut into bite-size cubes (about 2 cups)

½ cup freshly grated Parmesan cheese

½ teaspoon freshly ground black pepper

Make the pasta dough, and refrigerate.

Make the pesto, and set aside.

Remove the beans from the pod by pulling a thread that peels back on the curved side of the pod to release the beans inside. The beans have an outer skin that must be loosened. Place the beans into boiling water for 3 minutes. Drain and cool the beans for about 5 minutes, then remove the outer skin to reveal the fava beans that are now ready to cook.

In a medium pot filled one-half full of water, add ½ teaspoon salt and bring to a boil over medium-high heat. Add the beans, and blanch for 5 minutes, or until they are tender to the bite. Remove with a slotted spoon, and set aside. In the same pot, add the potatoes and cook for about 10 to 12 minutes, until tender. Remove with a slotted spoon and set aside.

Remove the pasta dough from the refrigerator, roll it out, and cut the pasta sheet into 5-inch-wide strips, then roll each strip like a jellyroll into a 3-inch-long log. Trim the ends of the roll to make them straight. Cut into ¼-inch-wide strips, starting on the right side of the log. Then toss the circles of pasta nests into semolina or corn flour, unfurling them into pasta nests. Continue down each log until you have 5 or 6 nests.

Fill a large pot three-quarters full of water, add ¼ cup salt, and bring to a rolling boil over high heat. Add the pasta and cook about 5 minutes, until al dente. Drain.

In a large serving bowl, scoop the pesto, then add the drained pasta, then the beans and potatoes, and gently toss to combine. Top with grated Parmesan, season with freshly ground pepper, and serve immediately.

GREENS AND RICOTTA-STUFFED TORTELLINI *with Walnut Pesto*

I find it very meditative to make pasta, because you have to roll it for 10 to 15 minutes, and this is a very Zen experience for me. I buy our flour directly from local mills, and luckily in the United States there are lots of resources for buying authentic 00 flour (see Source Guide, page 205). It's more finely ground than all-purpose flour and easier to work with. Making pasta is much easier than you think! ✂ *Serves 4*

For the filling:
1 tablespoon plus 1 teaspoon salt, divided
3 cups loosely packed baby kale
2 cups loosely packed baby arugula
½ cup loosely packed baby spinach
2 cups ricotta
½ cup freshly grated Parmesan cheese
½ teaspoon freshly ground black pepper
¼ teaspoon freshly grated nutmeg
1 large egg

For the walnut pesto:
1 cup shelled walnuts
½ clove garlic
2 tablespoons freshly grated Parmesan cheese,
plus ¼ cup for serving
½ cup extra virgin olive oil
¼ teaspoon salt

For the tortellini:
Basic Egg Pasta Dough (recipe, page 30)
¼ cup salt

To prepare the filling: Fill a medium pot three-quarters full of water and add 1 tablespoon salt. Bring to a boil over high heat. Fill a large bowl half full of ice water.

Add the kale, arugula, and spinach to the boiling water and blanch them quickly, for about 30 seconds to 1 minute. Remove the greens with a spider strainer and plunge into the ice water. Pour the greens into a colander, then press with a spoon to remove excess moisture.

Place the greens, ricotta, Parmesan, pepper, 1 teaspoon salt, and the nutmeg in a food processor fitted with a metal blade and blend until smooth, about 30 seconds. Add the egg and blend until it is well incorporated. Cover and refrigerate the mixture until you are ready to fill the tortellini. It will keep in the refrigerator for up to 1 day.

To prepare the pesto: Preheat the oven to 350°F.

Put the whole walnuts on a sheet tray, place it on the middle rack, and roast for 3 to 5 minutes, until the walnuts are golden brown. Do not let them burn. Set aside to cool.

When cool, finely chop the walnuts and set aside 2 tablespoons for the garnish. Combine the remaining walnuts and the garlic in a food processor and pulse for about 30 seconds. Add 2 tablespoons Parmesan, olive oil, and salt and blend for 30 seconds to 1 minute, until combined; the pesto should be a loose consistency and still contain walnut pieces—this is not a paste. This can be made ahead and will keep in the refrigerator for 2 weeks.

To prepare the tortellini: Make the pasta dough and roll out into 4 sheets. If you are using the hand-rolled method rather than a pasta machine, each of the 4 sheets will need to be about 4 by 12 inches. You will need a 2-inch diameter cutter to cut the pasta into rounds. Place the 4 pasta sheets on a lightly floured surface, working in batches if necessary. Using the pasta circle cutter, cut circles out of the sheets. I like to fill them about four at a time. Make sure you cover the remaining circles with a kitchen towel so they don't dry out.

Place the filling into a pastry bag, and squeeze a 1-inch dollop of filling into each circle of dough (or you can spoon a teaspoonful of filling onto the dough). When all the rounds are filled, dip a clean finger or small brush into a bowl of water and brush onto the pasta-filled circle to moisten around the filling. Fold the filled pasta circles in half, pressing gently along the edges to seal and form a half circle. On the straight side, take the two corners between your thumb and forefinger, bring them together, and press the corners together, being careful that the filling stays inside the tortellini. Work quickly so the pasta doesn't dry out.

Fill a large stockpot three-quarters full of water and bring to a boil over high heat. Add ¼ cup salt to the pasta water. When it comes to a full boil, reduce the heat to medium-low, maintaining a gentle boil. Drop the tortellini in the water and cook for 4 to 6 minutes. Remove using a slotted spoon or spider strainer and place them in a large mixing bowl. Toss with the pesto, then spoon the tortellini onto four bowls, top with ¼ cup grated Parmesan and the reserved chopped walnuts, and serve immediately.

CHESTNUT PASTA

Chestnut pasta is a hardy pasta with a bite that can hold a heavy sauce. On the other hand, you can enjoy the nutty flavor when it is simply tossed with olive oil and pecorino cheese. Chestnut pasta can also be cut into many other noodle shapes, such as tagliatelle or the traditional diamond shape for the local Lasagna Bastarda dish (recipe follows). Chestnut pasta has nice chewy bite, because chestnut flour is more dense—similar to a hazelnut flour. The chestnut flour is usually mixed with all-purpose flour to lighten the texture of the pasta. I had never worked with chestnut flour until I moved to Lunigiana. I absolutely love the flavor and highly recommend you try it. ✂ ***Serves 6 to 8***

2 cups all-purpose flour

1 ½ cups chestnut flour, sifted

1 teaspoon salt, plus ¼ cup for cooking the pasta

In the bowl of a standing mixer fitted with a dough hook, combine the all-purpose and chestnut flours and the salt, and blend on low speed. Add 1 to 1 ½ cups water gradually, just until the dough comes together to form a ball—you may not need all the water. Cover in plastic wrap and let rest for 45 minutes.

Transfer the dough to a well-floured board, and roll out to a 12 by 18-inch rectangle about ⅛ inch thick. To cut the traditional diamond shapes, I like to use the long edge of my rolling pin as a guide; place it on the dough from corner to corner to cut diagonally in one direction, then in the opposite direction to form a diamond shape. The diamond shape is used in this recipe as well as Testaroli (recipe, page 119). It appears to be the traditional shape of these 2 hand-cut pasta dishes. I have only seen this in Lunigiana.

Fill a large stockpot ¾ full with water and add the salt. Bring to a boil over high heat, add the pasta, and cook 5 minutes until al dente. Use a slotted spoon to transfer the pasta to a platter. Serve warm.

LASAGNA BASTARDA
with Spinach Pesto

This is a traditional dish from our region, and different versions can be found all over Tuscany. It is really not lasagna, which is why it's called "bastard" lasagna. The name isn't very poetic, but the dish is a beloved homemade pasta typical of northern Tuscany, particularly the Lunigiana and Garfagnano area, where sweet chestnuts are a staple food from late autumn to the end of spring. The pasta is cut into large diamonds, then tossed with the pesto. It can also be served with a ragù, walnut pesto (recipe, page 34), or La Fortezza Bolognese Sauce (recipe, page 143), if you prefer.

Serves 6 to 8

Chestnut Pasta (recipe, page 35)

6 cups loosely packed spinach leaves

1 cup grated Parmesan cheese, plus ¼ to ½ cup for serving

½ teaspoon salt

½ cup extra virgin olive oil, plus 1 to 2 tablespoons for drizzling on the finished pasta

1 cup blanched almonds

2 cloves garlic (optional)

Make the chestnut pasta.

While the pasta is coooking, in a food processor fitted with a metal blade, combine the spinach, 1 cup Parmesan, salt, ½ cup olive oil, almonds, and garlic (if using). Pulse for about 2 to 3 minutes until the pesto is smooth and fully combined.

Transfer the cooked pasta to a serving plate, top with pesto, drizzle with olive oil, and finish with Parmesan cheese. Serve warm.

LARDO

This salt-cured and spiced fatback is best defined as a condiment/salumi and uses an ancient method of preservation. It can be sliced thinly and put on Marocca di Casola (recipe, page 188) as an appetizer, or melted on shrimp on toast, or sliced and put into pastas. Younger chefs are using very creative salt rubs to cure their lardo. Once you taste it, you'll find lots of ways to use it. ❧ ***Makes 2 ½ pounds***

2 ½ pounds fresh, skinless pork fatback
¼ cup plus 1 tablespoons kosher salt
6 cloves garlic, minced
6 sprigs thyme
4 sprigs rosemary

2 tablespoons crushed black pepper
1 tablespoon ground coriander
1 teaspoon ground cinnamon
1 star anise, crushed

Cut the pork into 2 pieces and place it in a refrigerator container (see note below). Mix together the remaining ingredients—salt, garlic, and spices—to create the cure rub and rub it evenly over the meat.

Let cure in the refrigerator for 6 months.

Note: If you don't own a marble lardo box, the container should be a nonreactive glass container, wrapped in a black bag or dark cloth to shun excess light.

Each month, open and redistribute the cure over the pork, ensuring that all sides are covered.

After 6 months, rinse the pork and pat dry. Lardo can be wrapped in plastic wrap and stored in the refrigerator for up to 6 months.

SHRIMP WITH LARDO ON TOAST

Serves 4

2 medium tomatoes

8 spears asparagus, cut into 2-inch lengths

3 tablespoons extra virgin olive oil

4 basil leaves, cut into ribbons

½ teaspoon salt

½ teaspoon freshly ground black pepper

8 slices rustic bread

16 medium shrimp, cleaned and without heads

16 thin slices (2 by 3-inch rectangles) lardo, or you may substitute pancetta

Preheat the oven to 350°F.

Bring a pot of water to a boil over medium-high heat, then add the whole tomatoes and boil for a few seconds to loosen the skins. Remove carefully with a spider strainer, and use a knife to remove the skins. Dice the tomatoes, and set aside.

Keep the water at a boil and blanch the asparagus for 2 minutes, then remove with a spider strainer and plunge into a bowl of ice water to cool. Remove to drain on paper towels.

In a bowl, toss the asparagus, diced tomatoes, olive oil, basil, salt, and pepper.

Place the bread slices on a sheet pan, place 2 shrimp atop each slice, and a slice of lardo atop each shrimp. Bake in the oven for 5 minutes until the lardo is melted and the shrimp are pink. Top the toasts with a teaspoon of the tomato-asparagus mixture. Place on a platter, and serve.

Lardo comes from a famous town at the base of the Carrara marble quarries high up on a mountain of marble. The tiny hamlet of Colonnata is situated at 500 meters (1,640 feet) above sea level, and around 8 kilometers (5 miles) from Carrara on the coast. It is at the heart of the famous marble quarries of this corner of northwest Tuscany. Although probably not on the heart-friendly diets of most, a small slice of lardo on a hot piece of toast is a piece of buttery heaven, and Colonnata is the place to sample the best, identified by the mark "Lardo di Colonnata IGP" on the label. It's about thirty minutes from La Fortezza, so I buy lardo to use in many of our dishes. Good lardo is produced across all of Italy to keep up with demand.

It is made using the fatback of the pig, and is prepared by first cutting the meat and brining the individual pieces with salt and spices, such as star anise. The fatback is then placed inside a marble box. These marble boxes are the best way to cure the lardo. Always curious to try out new processes, I bought a vintage marble-curing box at a local flea market, and cleaned and sterilized it to use at home.

The process of seasoning and curing the fatback in salt—brining it—creates a unique microclimate to aid in curing the meat. The lardo should be a smooth consistency with layers of herbaceous flavor, melting in your mouth like butter on warm bread. It's actually quite an easy process; however, lardo is a testament to patience, because you need to cure it for six months.

POLENTA

Polenta is a side dish that is quintessentially Italian. It is finely or coarsely ground dried yellow corn, what we call grits in the South. It's a gloriously smooth creamy starch that goes well with meat or fish, and vegetables. It is a staple in the Italian home, and Lunigiana embraces it wholeheartedly. When I first moved here I would see corncobs hanging on a line very decoratively in front of houses. I thought that these garlands were ornamental until one day I told our chef how pretty they were and how much I liked them. He laughed and said, "Annette, these are people drying the corn to grind polenta." I was frankly a little embarrassed that I had not realized this. It never ceases to amaze me that people in the countryside make everything by hand. This is a basic recipe for polenta; you can grill or fry it once it's solidified in the refrigerator overnight. Its versatility makes it a perfect accompaniment to all sorts of dishes.

Serves 4 to 6

2 teaspoons kosher salt

2 cups quick-cooking polenta, medium or coarse-grain

1 teaspoon freshly ground black pepper

2 tablespoons unsalted butter, plus 1 tablespoon for the pan if chilling overnight

¼ cup extra virgin olive oil for grilling, or for skillet-frying

In a medium saucepan over medium-high heat, add 4 cups water and the salt, and bring just to a boil. Reduce the heat to low, and slowly whisk in the polenta, then season with pepper. Continue to whisk for about 2 to 3 minutes, until the mixture starts to tighten up; then quickly whisk in the butter until well combined and the polenta is very thick. Serve immediately.

For Grilling: Liberally butter a rimmed 15 by 13-inch sheet pan. Pour the hot polenta onto the pan, smooth it out with a spatula, and set aside to cool to room temperature. Cover with plastic wrap and refrigerate for 2 hours, or overnight, to set.

When you are ready to grill, cut the polenta into equal wedges, or cut circles using a biscuit cutter. Coat the pieces with olive oil. Place on a hot grill for 2 to 3 minutes on each side, to make grill marks. Serve warm.

For Frying: Liberally butter a rimmed 15 by 13-inch sheet pan. Pour the hot polenta onto the pan, smooth it out, and set aside to cool to room temperature. Cover with plastic wrap and refrigerate for 2 hours, or overnight, to set.

When you are ready to fry, cut the polenta into equal wedges, or cut circles using a biscuit cutter. Heat the oil in a large frying pan over medium heat, and place 4 pieces into the pan, making sure to leave room around each piece. Fry on each side for 3 to 4 minutes until browned and crispy. Drain on paper towels and serve warm.

BALSAMIC GRILLED MACKEREL
on Fried Polenta
(SGOMBRO CON POLENTA)

This traditional Lunigiana dish, called sgombro con polenta, *has been borrowed from a Venetian dish using sardines. A hundred years ago, it wouldn't be unheard of if a Venetian married into a Lunigiana family and had to use mackerel to replace the sardines in the recipe. Mackerel doesn't appear on menus often in America, but it's commonly used in Italy. This is a great way to use a plentiful fish that is also inexpensive and just plain good. The* aceto balsamico *(balsamic vinegar) in this recipe adds sweetness to the fish, and balances the tartness of the lemon. About two hours from La Fortezza is the city of Modena, the center of traditional balsamico—if it's from anywhere else it's not considered authentic. Note: You will need a lot of oil on the grill to prevent sticking. I like to use wood for flavor, but charcoal is fine too.*

ℵ *Serves 4*

Polenta (recipe, page 42)
2 medium mackerel (about 2 pounds), filleted, skin on
2 cloves garlic, minced
⅓ cup extra virgin olive oil
⅓ cup good-quality balsamic vinegar
1 teaspoon salt
1 lemon, cut in half, for the grill and for garnish

Make the polenta and refrigerate it.

Rinse and dry the fish. Combine the garlic, olive oil, vinegar, and salt in a zip-tight plastic bag. Place the fish into the bag to marinate, and refrigerate for 1 to 2 hours.

Prepare a grill for direct cooking, or preheat a gas grill to medium-high heat, 350 to 400°F. If using a charcoal grill, the grill is ready when the charcoal turns white, about 1 hour after lighting the coals. Clean your grate and let it heat at least 10 minutes before cooking.

When you are ready to grill, remove the fish from the marinade. Place the fish skin side down, and the lemon halves cut-side-down, on the grill and cook for 5 minutes. Carefully turn the fish over and cook an additional 5 minutes, until the flesh is firm and the skin is crisp.

Fry the polenta as directed in the recipe on page 42.

ROSEMARY-SMOKED BRANZINO

The location of Lunigiana, between the mountains and the sea, provides the perfect microclimate to enjoy all the bounties of the earth. It's a marvel, and a magical place. In the spring and summer, we frequently visit the Ligurian Sea, which is only a half hour drive from La Fortezza. It provides loads of entertainment and a bounty of seafood for our table. The nearby town of La Spezia is home to the Italian Navy, and is a bustling town. It has a busy fishing industry that provides the town and surrounding areas with an endless supply of local fish. I make weekly trips to the fish market. Nearby beach towns like Carrara, Massa, and Forte di Marmi offer interesting sites, such as the marble mines of Carrara. Forte di Marmi is known as the Hamptons of Tuscany. Forte (as it's called) is a gorgeous beach town filled with retro beach clubs and an amazing market in the main square held on Wednesdays and Sundays during the summer months.

Branzino is one of my favorite types of fish. It is flaky and subtle, and it takes on flavors quite well. Recently, I smoked it with rosemary from our garden. The results were a buttery, smoky flavor with a melt-in-your-mouth texture. When you buy branzino, ask your fishmonger to gut and clean it for you. If you can't find branzino, trout is a fine substitution. Note: On the English version of most Italian menus it's called sea bass, but it's really branzino.

Serves 4

---

3 whole branzino (about 2 pounds total)

2 tablespoons fresh chopped thyme

2 tablespoons coarsely chopped fresh rosemary

1 tablespoon salt

3 tablespoons extra virgin olive oil

3 lemons, 1 juiced and the rest thinly sliced

1 large bunch fresh rosemary stems, for the grill

Rinse the fish under cold water, pat dry, and place in a glass dish.

Combine the thyme, chopped rosemary, salt, oil, and the juice of 1 lemon in a small bowl, and massage this seasoning into the fish on both sides. Refrigerate, covered, for 1 hour.

Start your grill, and heat until the coals are white (about 1 hour). Stuff the cavity of each fish with slices of lemon, then place the fish on the grill, with a bunch of rosemary stems alongside, and close the grill lid. Smoke should start forming, but do not open the grill for 5 minutes. This will ensure the smoky flavor of the rosemary permeates the fish.

After 5 minutes, gently turn the fish and grill the other side for 10 minutes, uncovered. Add more rosemary if it has burned off. Watch to make sure the fish doesn't burn.

Remove the fish, garnish with slices of the remaining lemons, and serve warm.

PORK SAUSAGE-STUFFED RABBIT
with Sour Cherry Sauce

We have a lovely old sour cherry tree behind La Fortezza. One spring day while walking to the vineyard, I noticed it was heavy with fruit and I began thinking about how I could use the sour cherries in various dishes. Since rabbit is a favorite local dish around the region and at our house, a sour cherry sauce seemed perfect to serve with it. I came up with this recipe, and it has given us great pleasure—and ended up saving the old sour cherry tree.
Note: The saddle of the rabbit is the cut of meat that runs from the end of the rib cage to the hind legs, essentially comprising the two loins that sit on either side of the spine and the skin and muscle surrounding them.

Serves 4 to 6

For the rabbit:

4 ounces (about 10 slices) bacon, cut into
thin slices

1 saddle of rabbit (about 1 ½ pounds), deboned

8 ounces pork sausage, links or bulk, skin
removed

1 clove garlic, minced

1 teaspoon chopped fresh rosemary

2 tablespoons extra virgin olive oil

For the sour cherry sauce:

6 cups sour cherries, pitted and stems removed

1 cup red wine

1 cup sugar

2 tablespoons fresh lemon juice

1 teaspoon salt

Preheat the oven to 400°F.

To prepare the rabbit: Place a sheet of plastic wrap on a cutting board, and lay the bacon slices overlapping in a single, continuous fashion to form a rectangle larger than the rabbit saddle; you should have about 3 inches on each side of the rabbit saddle.

Prepare the rabbit saddle by placing it between two pieces of plastic wrap and pounding it with a meat mallet until it is ¾ inch thick. Then place the rabbit saddle on top of the bacon slices.

In a medium bowl, crumble the sausage with a fork, and mix with the minced garlic, rosemary, and oil. Evenly spread the sausage on top of the rabbit. Roll the rabbit-bacon-sausage package into a tight roll and secure it tightly with kitchen string in three places: in the middle, and about 1 inch from each end. Place in a large roasting pan and roast for 45 minutes, until the internal temperature reads 160°F on a meat thermometer.

Just before the rabbit has finished roasting, make the sour cherry sauce: In a small saucepan combine the pitted cherries, red wine, sugar, lemon juice, and salt over medium-high heat. Bring to

a boil, then reduce the heat to medium and simmer for 7 to 8 minutes, or until the cherries release all their juices. Keep warm until you are ready to serve. This sauce can be made 2 days ahead and gently reheated before serving. Leftover sauce will keep for 2 to 4 days in the refrigerator.

Remove the rabbit from the oven and let rest for 10 minutes, and remove the strings before cutting it into ¾-inch-thick slices. Serve warm and pass the warm sour cherry sauce around the table.

SAUSAGE AND KALE
(SALSICCIA E CAVOLO)

This easy, delicious supper is a no-brainer for me. With Italian sausage and fresh kale, it is simple fare. Because it is cooked in a cast-iron skillet, you could also add eggs (or cook them on the side) and serve it as a hearty brunch dish. Tuscan kale and chard are both popular ingredients in this region, and have been for a very long time. The local recipes with greens in them originally called for the wild field greens that the locals have eaten for centuries. I am always amazed by the resourcefulness of Italians when it comes to using what's literally at their feet, as well as their ability to identify any wild edible green, mushroom, flower, or herb. I have been hiking into the hills with friends who insisted on stopping and gathering field greens to take home for lunch. By the time we arrive home, we've usually picked armfuls.

Serves 4

3 tablespoons extra virgin olive oil

8 Italian sausages (about 2 pounds), sweet or hot

½ red onion, thinly sliced

6 cups cavolo (Tuscan kale), stems removed, leaves cut crosswise into 1-inch strips

1 teaspoon red pepper flakes, or to taste

3 cloves garlic, minced

1 teaspoon salt

½ teaspoon freshly ground black pepper

3 tablespoons fresh lemon juice

Marocca di Casola bread (recipe, page 188) or any store-bought rustic bread, for serving

In a large cast-iron skillet, heat the olive oil over medium heat and cook the sausages about 10 minutes, until they are brown; then remove and set them aside. Add the onion and sauté 3 minutes, until soft. Add the kale, hot pepper, garlic, salt, and black pepper and toss until just wilted; then drizzle with lemon juice. Serve the sausages atop the kale with the crusty bread.

BREADED AND DEEP-FRIED LAMB CHOPS
(COSTOLETTE DI AGNELLO FRITTE)

Fried lamb chops are to Lunigianesi what fried chicken is to Americans. This traditional lamb dish is pan-fried, not deep-fried, and the breading isn't heavy, so it's a perfect comfort food for lunch or for supper. I put this recipe in the nonna *(grandma) food category. Served with a little squeeze of lemon, it's a delicious dish that is frankly one of my favorites.* ✂ *Serves 4 to 6*

8 lamb chops, about ¾ inch thick

1 cup milk

2 large eggs

1 cup plain dried breadcrumbs

2 cups canola oil for frying, plus more if needed

1 teaspoon salt

1 lemon, cut into wedges

Soak the lamb chops in a bowl with the milk for about 1 hour before breading, to tenderize.

In a wide bowl, whisk the eggs. Place the breadcrumbs in a third bowl or on a plate.

Pat the lamb chops dry and dredge each chop in the egg mixture, then the breadcrumbs, covering the chop completely. Transfer to a plate as you continue to bread the remainder of the chops.

Heat the oil in a large frying pan or cast-iron skillet over medium-high heat. Place only 3 or 4 chops at a time in the pan, depending on their size, to allow even cooking, and fry for 3 to 5 minutes on each side until golden brown and crispy.

While the lamb chops are hot, drain on paper towels, sprinkle with salt, then transfer to a pan and keep warm on low heat in the oven while you finish cooking. Continue cooking the remaining chops in the same manner, adding more oil if needed.

Serve on a platter garnished with lemon wedges.

PAPPARDELLE WITH RABBIT RAGÙ

We eat a lot of rabbit at La Fortezza because rabbits are abundant in this region. Plus, rabbit is easy to cook, and the meat is delicate, tender, and flavorful—not gamey at all. Like many recipes in this book, this one can be traced to ancient times. I can imagine the soldiers being served this rabbit dish five hundred years ago, when this was a medieval fortress. For this recipe, you need 3 pounds of meat, so ask your butcher to order the rabbit for you and have them break it down. Discuss whether you will need to order two bone-in rabbits in order to get 3 pounds of meat.

Serves 4 to 6

---

1 (3-pound) rabbit, broken down into bone-in cuts

1 teaspoon salt, plus ¼ cup for cooking the pasta

½ teaspoon freshly ground black pepper

1 bottle red wine

2 teaspoons dried rosemary

2 teaspoons ground oregano

3 tablespoons extra virgin olive oil

8 ounces pancetta, diced (1 cup)

1 small onion, coarsely diced

1 carrot, coarsely diced

1 stalk celery, coarsely diced

1 tablespoon tomato paste

2 cloves garlic

4 cups beef stock

2 (14-ounce) cans Mutti Polpa chopped tomatoes, or another good-quality brand

Basic Egg Pasta Dough (recipe, page 30)

1 cup grated Parmesan cheese

Place the rabbit pieces in a bowl, season with salt and pepper, then add the red wine to cover. Add the rosemary and oregano; then cover and marinate in the refrigerator overnight.

The next day, remove the rabbit from its marinade, reserving the wine and herbs in the bowl. Pat the meat dry with paper towels and set aside on a plate.

Preheat the oven to 300°F.

Add the olive oil to a large Dutch oven over medium-high heat, and sear the rabbit pieces in batches, being careful not to crowd the pot, 3 to 4 minutes. As soon as they brown, remove and set aside on a plate. When all are browned, lower the heat to medium, add the pancetta, onion, carrot, and celery to the pot, and stir for about 5 minutes, until the onion is translucent.

Return the rabbit pieces to the pot, along with the tomato paste and garlic. Stir to combine, and add the beef stock and canned tomatoes; cook for 1 minute, then add the reserved red wine marinade.

Cover and roast in the oven for 3 hours, or until the meat is falling off the bones. Carefully remove the rabbit pieces from the stew, and use a fork or your fingers to pull the meat from the bones. The meat should be in small pieces; however, try and keep some larger pieces.

Return deboned meat to the pot; discard the bones. If the sauce needs thickening, simmer with the lid off for 30 minutes more, or until you have a perfect, rich ragù consistency.

While the ragù reduces, prepare the pasta dough and cut into ½-inch-wide pappardelle. Fill a large stockpot three-quarters full of water and bring to a boil over medium-high heat; add ¼ cup salt and the pasta and cook for about 5 minutes, until al dente. Drain the pasta well and transfer to a serving bowl. Top with the rabbit ragù and grated Parmesan. Serve warm.

SGABEI
(FRIED DOUGH)

Every region in Italy has a version of fried dough or pasta. Lunigiana's typical regional version is called sgabei (pronounced SCA-BAE). It is a yeasted dough, cut into rectangles, then fried and salted. The recipe originates from the Val di Magra near the Bay of Poets. It is said that the fried dough was made from leftover bread. Today it is served at our summer sagre, village festivals that highlight local specialties. These puffy pillows of goodness are best served warm with prosciutto, salami, and pecorino and stracciatella cheeses.

Makes 10

1 tablespoon active dry yeast

½ teaspoon salt, plus about 2 teaspoons for seasoning

4 cups plus 1 tablespoon 00 flour, sifted

3 cups olive oil, or enough for a depth of 1 inch in the pan, for frying

In the bowl of a standing mixer with the dough hook in place, briefly blend the yeast, ½ teaspoon salt, and 1 ½ cups water on low speed, allowing the hook just to mix the ingredients. Let the yeast bloom for 10 minutes. Once bubbles start to form, add the sifted flour and knead on medium speed until the mixture is smooth and soft. Transfer to a bowl, cover with a towel, and let the dough rise for 1 hour.

Roll out the dough and cut into 1 by 3-inch strips. Place on a cookie sheet and let the strips rise for 30 minutes.

In a large skillet or frying pan with high sides, heat the oil over medium-high heat to 375°F. Fry the strips in batches for 3 to 5 minutes, being careful not to crowd the pan, and flipping with tongs so they cook evenly, until they are crisp and light golden brown. Use a slotted spoon to transfer them to drain on paper towels, and salt them liberally. Serve warm with an assortment of charcuterie and cheeses.

GIOVANNA'S CHESTNUT FLOUR FRITTERS
with Ricotta and Chestnut Honey

By now you know more about Lunigiana and one of its favorite ingredients, chestnut flour. My friend Giovanna intro-
duced me to this amazing dessert when we first met. I remember trying them at our first lunch together at her argitur-
ismo farm and being bowled over by the taste. These warm, soft pillows topped with ricotta and drizzled with chestnut
honey are the perfect sweet and savory treat. They are easy to make and I can literally eat ten of them at a sitting.
Chestnut flour is truly the magical ingredient in this recipe.

Makes 8 to 10 fritters

---

4 cups canola oil, or enough for a depth of 1-inch in the pot, for frying

¼ cup all-purpose flour, sifted

1 cup chestnut flour (see Source Guide, page 205), sifted

1 teaspoon baking powder

½ teaspoon salt

½ teaspoon sugar

1 large egg, lightly beaten

1 cup sparkling water

1 tablespoon melted unsalted butter

1 cup fresh ricotta, for serving

Chestnut honey (see Source Guide, page 205), for drizzling

Heat at least 1 inch of oil in a Dutch oven, or deep fryer, to 365°F.

In a medium bowl, combine both flours, the baking powder, salt, sugar, and beaten egg. Stir in the sparkling water and melted butter, until the batter is smooth and free of lumps.

Drop ¼ cup batter at a time into the hot oil and fry for about 3 to 5 minutes, flipping with tongs every minute or two to ensure the fritters are golden brown overall. I like to fry just three at a time. Remove with a spider strainer or slotted spoon and drain on paper towels. Serve warm with a dollop of fresh ricotta and a drizzle of chestnut honey.

Artisanal Chestnut Flour Purveyor, Giovanna Zurlo

I met Giovanna online a few years ago after I geotagged La Fortezza on Facebook. I got a private message from her and she sent me a photo of La Fortezza she'd taken on her walk that day. She wondered who was doing the renovation, and was excited when she saw it tagged. I was pleased that she reached out and we made a plan to meet when I was again in Fivizzano.

I returned to Italy that spring, and soon Giovanna knocked on the door bearing gifts, like an Italian welcome wagon. Her basket held all of her homemade jellies, the chestnut honey she produces from her family's hives, and freshly milled chestnut flour from their forest—needless to say, I was thrilled.

Soon after she invited me to lunch. Giovanna made several dishes from their own chestnut flour, and my favorite were these warm chestnut fritters served with fresh ricotta and drizzled with homemade chestnut honey.

Ever since that lunch, Giovanna has been my Lunigiana slow food guide; in fact, she works as the regional Slow Food ambassador. I quickly enlisted her to share her knowledge and talk to our guests about the local fare available in the region. She shows up at La Fortezza with her car loaded with local products, and cooks with us, demonstrating fritters, and making her Grape Jam (recipe, page 151). I stock and use her chestnut flour year-round.

NADIA BONGI'S RICOTTA TIRAMISU

One day while we were picking up our usual order at Bongi Dairy, Nadia mentioned a tiramisu recipe she makes with her ricotta. Usually mascarpone is used to make this dessert, but she makes her tiramisu with the dairy's own fresh ricotta instead, whipping it by hand until smooth and fluffy. Intrigued, I asked her for the recipe—her version is so good, I'm sharing the recipe here. ✄ ***Serves 6***

3 large eggs, whites and yolks separated

¼ teaspoon salt

½ cup sugar

2 cups heavy cream, divided

16 ounces (2 cups) fresh ricotta

1 ½ cups freshly brewed espresso

¼ cup Marsala wine, or your choice of rum

24 crisp ladyfingers

2 tablespoons cocoa powder, for garnish

In the bowl of a stand mixer fitted with the whisk attachment, beat the egg whites and salt on high speed for about 6 to 8 minutes until soft peaks form. Transfer to a bowl and set aside.

Add the egg yolks and sugar to the mixer bowl and switch to the paddle attachment. Beat on medium speed until the custard is a pale yellow, about 2 minutes. Add 1 cup cream and beat 1 minute. With the mixer on low, add the ricotta and mix until smooth.

By hand, fold the whipped egg whites into the custard mixture.

In a small bowl, combine the espresso and Marsala.

Arrange 12 of the ladyfingers across the bottom of a 9 by 13-inch glass baking dish. Drizzle with half of the espresso mixture, then spread half the custard mixture on top. Lay the remaining 12 ladyfingers on top of the custard and drizzle with the remaining espresso mixture. Spoon the remaining custard on top of the ladyfingers to finish. Cover with plastic wrap and chill in the refrigerator for at least 4 hours.

Before serving, whip the remaining 1 cup cream. Spread the whipped cream across the top of the chilled tiramisu and dust with cocoa powder.

Cheese/Yogurt-maker, Nadia Bongi

I love to meet local food purveyors, so when a friend told me of Bongi Dairy, an organic dairy down the road, I visited that day. I took a ten-minute drive through olive groves behind La Fortezza. I found myself in gorgeous farmland, and up a narrow drive was a beautiful stone building. To the right were the milk cows, happily munching on fresh green grass and fragrant hay. Behind the main building was the office, retail space, and cheese-making room.

I was greeted by Nadia, a beautiful woman dressed head to toe in white, wearing a hair net and a beautiful smile.

"Do you want to see where we make the ricotta and the cheese?" she asked me in Italian. "Certo!" I responded.

The door to the cheese room was marked INGRESSO VIETATO, DO NOT ENTER. I entered anyway. The white tile room is a sterile environment with a giant cheese vat, where Nadia makes her exquisite yogurt and ricotta, as well as hard and soft cheeses, from their milk. Her cows are a variety called Alpine Brown, an ancient breed from the fifteenth century. Bongi Dairy is a generational business. Nadia has been working at the dairy her entire life—she's a master cheesemaker and annually attends the Slow Food cheese festival in Bra, in the Piedmont region, to show off her wares.

She pulled the ricotta from the simmering pot, placed the hot cheese into a form, and brought it out to the store so I could try it. There are not many things in life I enjoy more than fresh, warm ricotta. If you've never tried it, I highly recommend you do.

I get all of our dairy products from Nadia now, with the exception of Parmesan, which I source from Parma.

Estate

SUMMER
RECIPES

BRUSCHETTA
with Burrata and Pesto

This is one of my favorite easy recipes for aperitivo. We gather on the terrace around six-thirty in the evening for cocktails and nibbles, to enjoy the view and a glass of our wine, or an Aperol spritz. A local cheesemaker has the most divine burrata; it's smooth and oozes all over the pesto on the platter. Served with crusty, toasted bread, it's gone in about one minute flat. When you buy your burrata from the grocery, leave it out for an hour before you serve, so it softens. If you have leftover pesto in the fridge, this treat only takes minutes to assemble. I also discovered the leftover pesto burrata can be used to top pizza, and I sometimes add some zucchini blossom as well. It tastes amazing!

Serves 8 to 10

1 cup pesto (recipe, page 27)
1 baguette or Focaccia (recipe, page 89)
3 tablespoons extra virgin olive oil
1 ball fresh burrata cheese, at room temperature

Prepare the pesto and set aside.

Preheat the oven to 350°F.

Cut the baguette crosswise into 24 slices, 1-inch-thick, or 2 by 4-inch rectangles if using focaccia. Transfer to a baking sheet, brush with the oil, and bake for 5 to 8 minutes until golden brown.

Note: You can skip this step if using focaccia.

Place the burrata on a platter, slice it down the middle, and spoon the pesto into the cut. Serve with the bruschetta and a nice cocktail.

CROSTINI
with Galletti Mushrooms

We are very fortunate to have many mushroom hunters where we live in the country. Our sweet neighbor Cristian brings us handpicked mushrooms when he's been out and about in the countryside. Usually it's a big crate of delicate, bright yellow galletti mushrooms, also known as chanterelles. I hear him calling my name from the front of La Fortezza as he makes his way to our kitchen, where you will find me most days. The subtle, earthy flavor of the mushrooms, with the addition of a little balsamic vinegar and the sharp pecorino, makes this crostini a perfect two-bite appetizer.

Serves 4 to 6

¼ cup extra virgin olive oil

1 pound (6 cups) galletti or cremini mushrooms, roughly chopped

½ teaspoon salt

2 cloves garlic, minced

2 tablespoons balsamic vinegar

1 baguette or Focaccia (recipe, page 89)

10 slices pecorino cheese

¾ cup chopped fresh flat-leaf parsley

Preheat the oven to 350°F.

Heat the oil in a medium sauté pan over medium heat, and sauté the mushrooms, salt, and garlic, about 7 to 10 minutes, until the mushrooms are soft. Turn off the heat and toss with the balsamic vinegar.

Cut the baguette crosswise into 1-inch-thick slices, or cut the focaccia into 2 by 4-inch rectangles. Spoon the mushrooms on each slice of bread and top with a slice of cheese.

Place the crostini on a baking sheet and bake for 2 to 3 minutes, until the cheese is melted.

Garnish with parsley. Serve warm or at room temperature.

LA FORTEZZA MINESTRONE SOUP

With our amazing kitchen garden at La Fortezza, I have a wonderful selection of herbs and vegetables. The addition of farro or rice thickens this soup, making it close to a vegetable stew. You can serve it hot or at room temperature—it's good both ways. ✂ ***Serves 4 to 6***

2 ounces pancetta, finely diced

1 clove garlic, finely diced

1 small onion, finely diced

1 stalk celery, finely diced

¼ cup finely chopped fresh flat-leaf parsley

2 tablespoons extra virgin olive oil

2 carrots, cut into ¾-inch cubes

1 Yukon Gold potato, cut into ¾-inch cubes

2 zucchini, cut into ¾-inch cubes

1 teaspoon salt

½ teaspoon freshly ground black pepper

4 ripe tomatoes, diced

8 cups vegetable stock or water

1 ¾ cups shelled peas

1 ½ cups shredded kale (about half a bunch)

¾ cup shelled fresh borlotti beans

½ cup farro or long-grain rice

4 fresh sage leaves, chopped

½ cup chopped basil leaves

1 cup grated Parmesan cheese,

for serving

In a bowl, mix together the finely diced pancetta, garlic, onion, celery, and parsley.

Heat the oil in a large Dutch oven over medium heat. Add the pancetta mixture, carrots, potato, and zucchini. Season with salt and pepper. Sauté for 5 minutes until soft. Add the tomatoes and stock and bring to a boil over high heat, then reduce the heat to low and cook for 1 hour, or until the vegetables are tender.

Add the peas, kale, beans, and farro and simmer for another 45 minutes until the farro is soft. If you are using rice, simmer for 20 minutes, as rice cooks faster than farro.

Stir in the herbs and ladle into a soup tureen. Serve with crusty bread, and pass the Parmesan cheese around the table.

SCALLOPED POTATOES
with Tomatoes and Anchovy Parsley Sauce

Who doesn't love scalloped potatoes? This rustic recipe has no milk or cream in the ingredients, but it still bakes to a wonderful creamy texture. The paste made from the combined oil, tomatoes, anchovies, garlic, and parsley, layered with the soft potatoes, creates alchemy in the oven. Make sure the potatoes are thinly sliced, and that you buy good quality anchovies; they really make a huge difference in flavor. ✄ ***Serves 6 to 8***

....

5 tablespoons extra virgin olive oil, divided

2 medium yellow onions, thinly sliced

4 cups cherry tomatoes, sliced in half

½ teaspoon salt

1 (2-ounce) tin anchovies packed in olive oil

2 cloves garlic

2 tablespoons chopped fresh basil leaves

2 tablespoons fresh thyme leaves

¼ teaspoon freshly ground black pepper

1 cup chopped fresh flat-leaf parsley

¾ pound (about 2 to 3) Yukon Gold potatoes, sliced ¼ inch thick

1 cup grated Parmesan cheese

....

Preheat the oven to 400°F.

Place 3 tablespoons olive oil into a saucepan over low heat, add the onions, and sauté for about 3 minutes until tender. Fold the tomatoes into the onions, add salt, and cook for about 10 minutes, stirring occasionally, until the tomatoes soften and begin to break down. Set aside.

In a food processor, combine the anchovies with 1 tablespoon olive oil, the garlic, basil, thyme, pepper, and parsley. Pulse to make a loose paste and set aside.

Place half of the tomato-onion mixture in an even layer in the bottom of a 3-quart baking dish. Add 1 layer of potato slices, then spread the anchovy mixture over the slices, add another layer of potatoes, and top with the remaining tomato mixture. Sprinkle the top with 1 tablespoon olive oil, cover the dish with aluminum foil, and bake for 30 minutes. Remove from the oven and sprinkle the top with Parmesan cheese. Bake uncovered for 8 to 10 minutes, just until the cheese melts. Serve warm.

PICKLED ZUCCHINI, PEPPERS, AND EGGPLANT

This makes an easy, tasty side dish anytime, and is a great way to preserve summer's bounty for winter enjoyment. I pickle the vegetables whole whenever possible, or cut them to just fit the jar, because they're so impressive on the plate, and the vegetables retain their own flavors better. ✂ ***Makes two (1-pint) 16-ounce jars***

6 small zucchini (no more than 4 inches long)

2 small Italian eggplant (no more than 4 inches long)

2 red bell peppers

2 yellow bell peppers

1 ½ cups white vinegar

1 teaspoon salt

2 tablespoons sugar

3 tablespoons fresh whole oregano leaves

3 tablespoons fresh whole mint leaves

Prepare a grill for direct cooking, or preheat a gas grill to medium-high, about 400°F. If using charcoal, the grill is ready when the charcoal turns white, or 1 hour after lighting the coals. Clean your grate and let it heat at least 10 minutes before cooking.

When the grill is ready, place the whole zucchini, eggplant, and peppers directly on the grill and cook evenly, turning with tongs, for a total of 15 to 20 minutes, until the vegetables are charred. The zucchini will probably cook a bit faster than the eggplant and peppers. As the vegetables attain an overall char, transfer them to a platter to cool.

Cut the stems off the zucchini and eggplant. If you are using large eggplant, you will want to cut them at this point to fit the jars.

Transfer the peppers to a zip-tight bag, or place in a bowl and cover with plastic wrap. Let steam for about 10 minutes, and transfer to a cutting board. Gently remove the stems from the peppers and let any juice drain out. With your hands, peel off the skins (which should slip off easily after steaming). Cut each pepper in half and remove the ribs and seeds.

In a bowl, combine the zucchini, eggplant, and peppers.

In a saucepan, cook the vinegar, salt, and sugar over low heat for 3 minutes, just until the sugar dissolves, then set aside to cool. Pour the cooled brine over the vegetables. Stir in the oregano and mint leaves and let the brine steep at room temperature for at least 8 hours, or overnight.

When you are ready to fill the jars, first run the jars and their lids through a hot cycle on your dishwasher to sterilize.

Divide the vegetable mixture and brine evenly between the prepared jars. Close the lids tightly and refrigerate 1 week before serving. This is a quick pickling method, so the jars will need to be refrigerated, and will keep for up to 3 months.

SWEET AND SOUR PEPPERS IN OIL
(PEPERONI IN AGRODOLCE SOTT'OLIO)

Domenica Marchetti is a cookbook author and food writer who taught a workshop at La Fortezza on preserving Italy's foods; she kindly let me use her recipe for this book. The peppers keep at least three months in the refrigerator, which is a lovely way to enjoy them all winter long. I keep at least one jar on hand at all times to add to pizzas, frittatas, summer pasta dishes, or rice salads. They go with almost anything from the grill—bistecca, sausages, lamb chops, swordfish, or tuna. Because the peppers are cured in oil rather than in vinegar brine, I don't process them in a hot-water bath.

Makes two 1-pint (16-ounce) jars

8 ripe bell peppers, in a mix of colors

2 tablespoons nonpareil capers, rinsed and drained

2 tablespoons finely chopped fresh flat-leaf parsley

1 cup white wine vinegar

¼ cup sugar

1 ½ teaspoons fine sea salt

2 cloves garlic, sliced paper-thin

About 4 cups extra virgin olive oil, for filling the jars

Preheat the broiler. Broil the peppers on a rimmed baking sheet about 4 inches from the broiler for 10 to 15 minutes, turning with tongs every few minutes, until blistered and starting to blacken on all sides. (You can also char the peppers on a grill.) Transfer the peppers to a zip-tight bag, or cover in a bowl with plastic wrap, and let steam for about 10 minutes.

Transfer to a cutting board. Gently remove the stems from the peppers and let any juice drain out. With your hands, peel off the skins (which should slip off easily after steaming). Cut each pepper in half and remove the ribs and seeds. Slice lengthwise into thin strips or dice, as preferred. Transfer the peppers to a heatproof bowl and stir in the capers and parsley.

In a saucepan, bring the vinegar, sugar, salt, garlic, and 1 cup water to a boil over medium-high heat. Boil for 2 minutes to dissolve the sugar, and then pour over the pepper mixture. Let steep for 1 hour at room temperature.

Wash the jars and lids and sterilize by boiling them for 10 minutes in a large pot of water. Remove from the water and let air-dry.

Drain the peppers, reserving about ½ cup of the brine. Pack the peppers into the prepared jars then pour 1 tablespoon brine over each. Fill each jar with enough olive oil to submerge the peppers completely. Cover tightly and let the peppers sit at room temperature for 24 hours.

Keep in the refrigerator up to 3 months. Bring the peppers to room temperature before serving. Add more oil as needed to keep the peppers submerged.

Master Gardener, Gianluca Di Antonia

When we bought La Fortezza, we were introduced to the man who had cared for the property for many years. My first impression was that Gianluca was a slight man and seemed like a shy soul. He had kind eyes that were as blue as the summer sky. He smiled upon meeting me. He only speaks Italian, so we conversed in Italian about what I imagined for my garden in the future. I assured him he could stay on and work with me to make the grounds fruitful and beautiful. Now, years later, he continues to put his mark on the land. He mows the grounds and prunes the trees—but that is the least of what he does for La Fortezza. He tutors me about nature and the cycles of our grounds, and the plants and animals that live on these many acres. He has planted three hundred olive trees that will fruit eventually. He has nursed the fruit orchard back to life, doted over the ancient grape vines, and harvested the tiny yellow plums that I turn into liqueurs and jams. His pride and joy is the kitchen garden; he makes sure it provides lots of food for our kitchen year-round. I can honestly say he is the most important person on the grounds and the reason we eat so well here. I could not live without Gianluca, and neither could La Fortezza.

CHARD TART
(TORTA D'ERBI/ERBAZZONE)

Here in Lunigiana, and in nearby regions like Liguria, vegetable pies are a staple. Torta d'erbi is a classic regional dish found in every specialty store, in grocery stores, on restaurant menus, as well as on every table here. Everyone has a vegetable garden, there are flour mills nearby, and many people keep chickens, so vegetable pies are a natural dish. The name of this recipe translates to "herb tart," because the Italians colloquially refer to the wild greens picked in fields, including chard, as herbs. Erbazzone is another term for the tart; it implies "lots of greens." ✂ ***Serves 6 to 8***

For the tart crust:

1 ½ cups all-purpose flour, plus more for dusting the work surface

3 tablespoons extra virgin olive oil

7 tablespoons unsalted butter

½ teaspoon salt

For the filling:

5 tablespoons extra virgin olive oil, divided

2 tablespoons unsalted butter

2 ounces pancetta, diced (¼ cup)

1 large red onion, thinly sliced

8 cups loosely packed chopped chard leaves

1 clove garlic, minced

½ teaspoon salt

¼ teaspoon freshly ground black pepper

1 cup chopped fresh flat-leaf parsley

1 cup grated Parmesan cheese

Preheat the oven to 350°F.

To prepare the crust: Place the flour, oil, butter, and salt in the bowl of a standing mixer fitted with a paddle blade. On the low setting, slowly add ¼ cup warm water and mix until the dough forms a ball, about 5 minutes. Remove the dough, divide it in half to form 2 disks, wrap them in plastic wrap, and refrigerate for 30 minutes.

To prepare the filling: Heat 3 tablespoons oil and the butter in a medium saucepan over medium heat. Add the pancetta and cook for 3 minutes. Add and cook the onion until soft, about 3 minutes. Add the chard, garlic, salt, and pepper and stir until the chard has wilted, about 5 minutes. Remove from heat and set aside to cool.

Once the mixture has cooled, stir in the chopped parsley and Parmesan cheese and set aside at room temperature.

Once the dough has rested, prepare a lightly floured work surface. Roll out both disks of dough into 10-inch rounds, ¼ inch thick, and press one disk into the bottom of a 9 ½-inch springform pan. Place the chard mixture on top of the dough, distributing it evenly.

Place the second dough round over the filling to cover. Seal the crusts all around, pinching them together with your fingers or pressing with a fork, and brush the top crust with the remaining 2 tablespoons olive oil. Use a fork to prick the top all over, and then use a knife to cut 4 slits in the center.

Bake for 30 to 40 minutes, until the crust is golden brown.

Serve warm or at room temperature. It will last for a couple days sitting out on your counter, simply wrapped in foil or plastic.

RICOTTA AND CHARD-STUFFED CAPPELLETTI IN TOMATO SAUCE

The word cappelletti *means "little hats," which is what their shape resembles. Cappelletti are a type of stuffed fresh pasta originating from the northern Italian region of Emilia-Romagna, next-door neighbor to Lunigiana. These date back to the Middle Ages, when they were considered a luxury food for aristocrats' tables. They use the same ingredients as tortellini; the difference is the shape. They are an easy pasta to make. If you want to double the recipe, they freeze well up to 3 months. Just toss the frozen cappelletti into boiling water—they float to the top when done.* 🦎 *Serves 4*

Basic Egg Pasta Dough (recipe, page 30)

¼ cup salt, for cooking the pasta

Flour, for the work surface

For the tomato sauce:

3 tablespoons extra virgin olive oil

1 small onion, chopped

1 (28-ounce) can Mutti Polpa chopped tomatoes, or another good-quality brand

3 cloves garlic, minced

3 tablespoons dried oregano

3 tablespoons chopped fresh basil

½ teaspoon salt

For the filling:

2 cups stemmed and cleaned chard

1 ½ cups ricotta

1 cup grated Parmesan cheese

½ teaspoon salt

½ teaspoon freshly grated nutmeg

¼ cup grated Parmesan cheese, for serving

Prepare the pasta dough according to instructions.

To prepare the sauce: In a saucepan over medium heat, add the oil and onion and cook for 3 minutes, until the onion is translucent. Add the tomatoes, garlic, oregano, basil, and salt and stir. Reduce the heat to low and simmer for 2 hours, stirring occasionally so the sauce doesn't stick to the bottom of the pot. This can be made 2 days ahead and reheated for fresh pasta, or it will keep up to 6 months in the freezer.

To prepare the filling: Bring a pot of water to a boil over high heat; then add the chard and blanch for 2 or 3 minutes. Drain and let cool enough to handle. Squeeze to remove excess water, dry with a cloth towel, and finely chop. Transfer the chopped chard to a mixing bowl and add the ricotta, Parmesan, salt, and nutmeg; stir well to combine.

To assemble: Prepare a well-floured work surface and roll out a thin sheet of pasta. Use a round cookie cutter (you could also use a round raviolo stamp, or a fluted-edge rolling pasta cutter) to cut out 2-inch-diameter circles of dough.

Place 1 level teaspoon of stuffing in the middle of each circle. Using your fingertip or a pastry brush, moisten the edges of the circle with a little water so they will seal. Fold the circles in half over the filling to form half-moons, and press down the edges to seal the pastry. Then pull the two corners toward each other; this pinching motion should be under the filling (not above the filling as the tortellini is made), overlapping one over the other, and press down on the tips to help them adhere. Continue to do this until all of the cappelletti are made.

Fill a large pot with water, add the salt, and bring to a rolling boil over high heat. Add the cappelletti; once the pasta rises to the top, in about 5 minutes, remove with a spider strainer and place into bowls.

Top with the sauce and Parmesan and serve hot.

BREADED SOLE
with Dried Capers

Italians use capers in many of their dishes. I found Sicilian dried capers in a store near us in Modena, so I started using them instead of the ones packed in oil. If you crush dried capers, they can be used to flavor dishes more uniformly. I sprinkle them over the cooked fish to add that salty, sour flavor I love. Traditional brined capers, drained and patted dry, will also work. Instead of sole, you may substitute flounder or fluke with equal success.

Serves 4

8 small sole fillets (about 1 ½ pounds)

½ cup all-purpose flour

½ cup grated Parmesan cheese

¼ teaspoon salt

¼ teaspoon freshly ground black pepper

2 large eggs

3 cups fresh breadcrumbs

About ⅔ cup extra virgin olive oil, for frying

3 tablespoons unsalted butter

¼ cup dried capers, plus 3 tablespoons for garnish

1 lemon, cut into wedges

On a cutting board, check the fillets for bones and pat dry with paper towels. On a dinner plate or in a shallow dish, combine the flour, Parmesan cheese, salt, and pepper. In a bowl, lightly beat the eggs with a fork then stir in 3 tablespoons water. Place the breadcrumbs on another dinner plate.

One at a time, dredge a fillet into the flour mixture to cover all sides, then shake off the excess. Dip into the egg mixture to coat, then into the breadcrumbs. Press lightly on the breadcrumbs to adhere. Once the fillets are coated, transfer to a plate.

In a large cast-iron skillet, heat ⅓ cup of the oil over medium heat. Add 3 or 4 breaded fillets, careful not to crowd the pan. Fry for 2 minutes on one side until golden brown, then carefully turn the fillets and fry 1 ½ minutes on the other side until golden brown. Set the cooked fillets on a platter lined with paper towels to drain, then repeat with the remaining fillets. It may be necessary to add more oil.

Wipe the skillet with a paper towel and add the butter over low heat. Swirl it around until it starts to foam, then add ¼ cup capers. Cook for 1 or 2 minutes until the butter is a light caramel color, being careful not to burn it. Pour the caper butter over the fish. Crush the remaining 3 tablespoons dried capers and sprinkle them over the fish. Serve warm with lemon wedges.

SALT COD FRITTERS
with Sautéed Broccoli Rabe
(FRITTELLE DI BACCALÀ CON RAPINI ROSOLATI)

Salted cod isn't regularly used by American home cooks, but it's easy to find and not too difficult to prepare. It's a time-consuming process, but worth it in the end because you wind up with a melt-in-your-mouth fish fritter. The most involved part of preparation is that you have to soak the fish for 2 to 3 days before cooking. It's important not to skip this step. It's a commitment, like brining. This is a typical countryside recipe that derives from a "slow food" approach that also includes pickling, preserving, brining, curing, and soaking ingredients to use in the kitchen.

Serves 4

1 pound baccalà (salted cod)

1 cup sparkling water, at room temperature

1 tablespoon crumbled brick yeast

1 cup 00 flour, available in most groceries

½ teaspoon sugar

1 teaspoon salt, divided

3 cups canola oil, for frying, plus 3 tablespoons, for sautéing

2 tablespoons unsalted butter

4 cups (about 1 pound) broccoli rabe (rapini), cleaned and cut into 2-inch pieces

1 lemon cut into wedges, for garnish

The best method for soaking is to cover the baccalà with approximately 2 inches of cold water in a large bowl. Cover and refrigerate for up to 3 days, changing the water at least twice a day. It becomes softer the longer you soak it.

When you are ready to cook, prepare the batter. In a bowl, whisk together 1 cup sparkling water and the yeast, and set aside 10 minutes until bubbles form.

Whisk the yeast mixture into the flour until just combined, then whisk in the sugar and ½ teaspoon salt. Once well mixed, cover the bowl with plastic wrap and set aside for about 30 minutes. You will notice that the batter will have a slight foamy appearance—that is good.

Drain and dry the baccalà on paper towels and, with your hands, break the fish into approximately 3- to 4-inch pieces.

Add 3 cups canola oil to a nonstick frying pan over high heat. Use tongs to dip the fish pieces into the batter and fry them in two batches until both sides of the fish are golden, about 3 to 5 minutes each side. Drain the fish on paper towels.

Heat 3 tablespoons oil in another nonstick frying pan over medium heat, add the butter, the broccoli rabe, and the remaining ½ teaspoon salt and sauté for about 5 minutes until crispy.

Serve the baccalà fritters and crispy broccoli rabe together on a platter and garnish with lemon wedges.

BRAISED RABBIT
with White Balsamic Fig Sauce
(CONIGLIO AI FICHI)

We eat tons of figs from several fig trees on the property, and make our own fig jam, too. They ripen in late spring through early fall. Summer figs are bright green, and the trees that ripen in fall produce dark burgundy fruit, like Mission figs. Wild boars like to eat the low-hanging fruit, so we have to harvest them fast before the lower limbs are devoured by the beasts of the forest! The green figs are called Italian honey figs, which are similar to American Celeste figs, but you can substitute others that are available in summer. ✄ Serves 4 to 6

For the rabbit:

2 sprigs fresh sage

3 sprigs fresh rosemary

2 sweet onions, finely diced, divided

1 head garlic, cut in half

1 bottle dry white wine, ¼ cup reserved

2 tablespoons kosher salt

2 (1 ½-pound) rabbits, each broken down
into 6 to 8 bone-in cuts

¼ cup extra virgin olive oil

1 pint fresh figs (Mission figs, yellow figs,
or Celeste figs)

3 cups vegetable broth

For the fig sauce:

4 tablespoons unsalted butter

1 pint Mission figs

½ teaspoon salt

3 tablespoons white balsamic vinegar

⅓ cup vegetable broth

To prepare the rabbit: In a blender, place the sage, rosemary, half the diced onions, the garlic, wine, and salt and process until combined. Transfer the marinade to a large zip-tight bag. Add the rabbit pieces and refrigerate overnight.

Preheat the oven to 325°F. Remove the rabbit from the marinade and pat dry with paper towels. Discard the marinade.

Heat the olive oil in a large Dutch oven over medium-high heat for 1 minute, then brown the rabbit, a couple of pieces at a time so you don't crowd the pan, 5 to 8 minutes per side. Continue until all the pieces have browned; set aside.

Add the remaining diced onion to the pan and cook for 1 to 2 minutes, until the onions are translucent. Add the whole figs to the pan and cook for about 2 minutes, stirring occasionally, until the figs are soft and caramelized. Deglaze the pan by adding the ¼ cup reserved wine and the broth and scraping down the sides of the pan; then add the rabbit, cover, and bake in the oven for 45 to 50 minutes, until the rabbit is fork tender. While the rabbit bakes, make the sauce.

To make the fig sauce: In a medium sauté pan, melt the butter over medium-high heat. When the butter starts to brown, add the whole figs and cook for 5 minutes, stirring, until browned. Add the salt, then remove the figs from the pan and set aside. Lower the heat to medium, add the balsamic vinegar to the pan, and cook for about 20 seconds, stirring, until just warmed, then add the broth and heat for another 2 to 3 minutes to combine the flavors. Add the figs back to the pan and set aside until you are ready to plate the rabbit.

Place the rabbit on a platter and top with the fig sauce. Serve immediately.

GRILLED STEAK
with Arugula, Fresh Tomatoes, and Shaved Parmesan
(TAGLIATA DI MANZO CON RUCOLA E POMODORINI)

*This original Tuscan dish is one of the most popular meals I serve at La Fortezza. It is the very definition of local.
We have a butcher down the road who specializes in* bistecca, *or* tagliata di manzo *(this literally means "cut of beef").
He even has his own herd of cattle in the pasture behind his shop. I also buy from Modesto, the butcher whose meat
comes from Emilia-Romagna, and those cows are fed the rinds of Parmesan cheese. I'm not sure if this is the reason, but
that meat is amazingly rich and delicious. This steak is cut about 1 ½ inches thick, and grilled over a wood fire,
or I cook them in the forno (a wood-burning pizza oven). I dress the grilled steak with sweet ripened tomatoes from our
kitchen garden, and Parmesan cheese from nearby Parma (where Parmigiano Reggiano is made).
I drizzle it with fresh olive oil from our olive grove.* Molto Buono! 🦌 ***Serves 4***

---

2 (1 ½-pound) porterhouse steaks, 1 ½ inches thick (or 3 fingers thick, as we like to say in Italy)

2 tablespoons salt

1 tablespoon freshly ground black pepper

8 cups loosely packed arugula

4 ripe tomatoes, cut into wedges

¼ cup extra virgin olive oil

1 teaspoon Maldon flake salt, to finish

1 large chunk (about 6 to 8 ounces) Parmesan cheese, for shaving

---

Pat the steaks dry with paper towels, and salt and pepper them on all sides. Let stand at room temperature for 30 minutes before grilling.

Prepare a grill for direct cooking, or preheat a gas grill to 400 to 450°F (it's best to cook steaks on high heat). If using a charcoal grill, the grill is ready when the charcoal turns white, or 1 hour after lighting the coals. Clean your grate and let it heat at least 10 minutes before cooking.

Place the steaks on the grill and use a meat thermometer to check for your preferred doneness: 135°F for medium rare, 140°F for medium, and 145°F for medium well. Transfer the steaks to a cutting board to rest for 5 minutes before carving. Cut the steaks into ¼-inch-thick slices, on a slight angle.

Arrange the arugula and tomatoes on a platter, place the steak atop the arugula, drizzle with olive oil, and finish with Maldon flake salt. Use a vegetable peeler to shave Parmesan strips over the steaks. Serve immediately.

SAUTÉED SAUSAGE
with Charred Friggitelli Peppers

Friggitelli peppers are small green peppers with a slightly bitter flavor that pair well with sweet sausage and caramelized onions. This is a great topping for pizza, sandwiches, or as a meal in itself. Whether pan-fried or baked, the friggitelli are delicious for a lunch on crusty bread, with a bit of cheese and a glass of crisp white wine.

Serves 6 to 8

1 ½ pounds Italian friggitelli sweet peppers or Greek golden pepperoncini peppers,
available at most groceries

3 tablespoons plus 2 teaspoons extra virgin olive oil

1 small red onion, sliced

½ teaspoons salt

2 ½ pounds (about 8) sweet Italian sausages

Clean and dry the peppers and place them into a dry cast-iron skillet over medium heat. Using tongs to turn them, heat the peppers for 5 to 8 minutes until they are wilted and blackened, then transfer to a plate and set aside to cool. (You can also blacken the peppers on a grill.)

Place the olive oil and onion into the skillet, reduce the heat to low, and sauté the onion for about 20 minutes, until it is caramelized. Set aside to cool.

Clean the cooled peppers, removing the seeds and ribs. Toss the onion, peppers, and salt in a bowl and set aside.

In the same cast-iron skillet over medium heat, working in 2 batches so as not to overcrowd the pan, cook the sausages for 7 to 10 minutes, turning them so that they cook on all sides. Repeat for the second batch.

Slice the sausages, and serve topped with the peppers and onion.

SOFT AND HARD PANIGACCI

Panigacci is a specialty bread created in the town of Podenzana in Lunigiana. The story goes that during World War II the bridge connecting Podenzana to the food supply in nearby Aulla was bombed, and so when food became scarce they started making flatbread out of flour and water. With a little oil and cheese this became a main food source until food could once again be acquired. Panigacci remained a staple, and was traditionally paired with salumi and cheeses. The soft version is much like a crepe, and the hard version like a flatbread. I like to call them Italian tacos. Crispy yet pliable, hard panigacci are served with meats, soft cheese like stracciatella, or with vegetables inside, and with various savory toppings, like ragù and pesto, or simply olive oil, and Parmesan cheese on the side.

In the tiny town of Luni on the outskirts of Carrara, there is a special place to eat a panigacci—Ristorante Baracchetta, which serves cucina tipica, or local cooking. It is a homespun setting, and you just know that Mamma is back there in the kitchen. I have tried to re-create her recipe here. One day they invited me to the cucina, and I was given a very brief peek at their kitchen while they were preparing the panigacci. I wanted the recipe, but they told me it was made of only flour and water! As I have said, Italians are sometimes secretive about their recipes. After lots of visits and tries in my own kitchen, I was able to reconstruct their recipe. If you're near Cararra, stop in Luni to see this ancient Roman port and amphitheater, and enjoy lunch in the open air. You may ask yourself where the port is, because Luni is an inland city. Over hundreds of years Luni slowly became submerged and wetland covered the ancient city. All that remains is the amphitheater—and some fabulous panigacci. 🜨 ***Makes 12 to 14***

....

Soft panigacci:

1 ½ cups all-purpose flour

½ cup whole wheat flout

1 teaspoon salt

2 tablespoons extra virgin olive oil

Hard panigacci:

2 ¾ cups 00 flour

1 ½ teaspoons salt

½ teaspoon extra virgin olive oil

....

To make Soft Panigacci: Prepare your choice of toppings (see headnote).

Sift the flours into a bowl with the salt, and whisk in the oil and 2 cups water for at least 3 minutes, until all are very well incorporated. The batter will be very loose.

Heat a 10-inch cast-iron skillet on medium heat and ladle in ½ cup batter. Cook until light brown, 3 minutes per side. Repeat with the remaining batter. Serve warm, with your choice of toppings.

To make Hard Panigacci: In a food processor fitted with the dough blade, combine the flour, salt, and 2 ½ cups water, and blend completely for 1 to 2 minutes.

Use a paper towel to coat the bottom of a cast-iron skillet with the oil and set over medium heat. Once the skillet is hot, pour ¼ cup of the batter into the hot pan. Cook one side until brown, about 3 ½ to 4 minutes; when the edge of the panigacci begins to raise off the pan, flip it, and place a heavy pan on top to keep the panigacci flat. Cook 1 minute and remove from the pan. The surface may be blackened a bit, which adds to the authentic fire-cooked flavor. Wipe the pan with paper towel to remove any charred bits. Repeat with the remaining batter. Serve warm, with fillings.

FOCACCIA

I make this bread every day, and have taught hundreds of guests over the years how to follow this easy recipe. We eat it with meals, for sandwiches, and make breadcrumbs out of the stale leftovers—there's never any thrown out. It's crispy on the outside and soft and delicate on the inside, making it a great vehicle for sopping up sauces. Italians put their focaccia on the end of their fork and use it to sop up the sauce. This practice is called a scarpetta *in Italian, meaning "a little shoe." Focaccia is best eaten warm out of the oven, but definitely the same day.*

Makes one (13 x 15-inch) loaf

1 envelope (2 ¼ teaspoons) active dry yeast

4 cups 00 flour, plus ¼ cup for kneading

¾ cup extra virgin olive oil, divided, plus more for the baking sheet

1 tablespoon coarse salt, plus 2 teaspoons for finishing

In a large bowl, combine the yeast with ⅓ cup warm water and set aside 10 minutes until bubbles form.

Stir the flour, 1 cup water, ½ cup oil, and 1 tablespoon salt into the proofed yeast to form a soft, very sticky dough.

Oil a baking sheet well and use your fingers to spread the dough, stretching it gently into the corners to fill the entire sheet. Lightly oil your fingertips and poke dimples into the top of the dough.

Let the dough rest for 1 hour at room temperature, then repeat the process of poking dimples into the risen dough. Let the dough rest for another 30 minutes. Each time the dough will puff up.

When you are ready to bake, preheat the oven to 400°F.

Drizzle the top of the dough with 3 tablespoons olive oil and 3 tablespoons water, then sprinkle with 1 teaspoon coarse salt. Transfer the baking sheet to the oven and bake 30 minutes until golden brown.

Immediately out of the oven, drizzle the focaccia with remaining 1 tablespoon olive oil and 1 teaspoon salt to finish, and let cool slightly. Serve warm or at room temperature.

CHICKPEA PANCAKE
(FARINATA)

I used to eat lots of farinata when I lived on the Italian Riviera, where it's served in a big iron skillet. This gluten-free treat falls somewhere between a flatbread or skillet bread and a pancake. It's a good starchy accompaniment to eggs for brunch, alongside a salad for lunch, or as a tasty aperitivo with cocktails. It's easy to make, and a delicious alternative to focaccia for gluten-free guests. ✻ ***Makes one (12-inch) pancake***

1 cup chickpea flour, available at most groceries

2 tablespoons extra virgin olive oil, plus more for cooking and finishing

1 teaspoon salt

Freshly ground black pepper

In a large bowl, slowly whisk 1 ¾ cups water into the chickpea flour until combined. Stir in 2 tablespoons oil and salt. Cover with plastic wrap and let the batter rest at room temperature for at least 1 hour, or up to 12 hours.

When you are ready to bake the pancake, preheat the oven to 400°F.

Heat 1 tablespoon olive oil in a 12-inch cast-iron skillet over medium-high heat. When the oil is hot, add the batter—it will cover the bottom of the skillet.

Transfer the skillet to the oven and bake for 20 to 30 minutes. After about 20 minutes, check doneness by inserting a knife in the center of the pancake to see if it comes out clean. If the top has not yet browned, set it under the broiler for 1 or 2 minutes.

Let cool completely, then transfer the farinata to a platter or cutting board. Cut into wedges, drizzle with additional olive oil, and top with a ridiculous and obscene amount of coarsely ground black pepper. Serve warm.

FOCACCETTE DI AULLA

This recipe is from Aulla, a city about thirty minutes from La Fortezza. Focaccette are small, round focaccia. Italians have a million different types of bread, and this is simply a small version of focaccia. Enjoy these for breakfast, lunch, or as an aperitivo snack with local salumi and cheeses. In the city of Aulla there is a festival, a sagra, devoted to these small focaccia. They are made with corn flour, which makes them special. It may seem like there are a lot of variations of focaccia and there are, but to each city and each region, their specific focaccia is unique. It's one of the things I find very endearing. Each city and every family is very protective of their traditional breads.

✖ *Makes 8 small loaves*

1 tablespoon crumbled brick yeast

1 cup 00 flour

1 cup corn flour

¼ cup extra virgin olive oil, divided

1 teaspoon salt

In a bowl, combine the yeast with ⅓ cup warm water and set aside for 10 minutes until bubbles form.

Mix the two flours in a separate bowl.

Once the yeast has bloomed, add it to the bowl of a standing mixer fitted with a dough hook, along with 3 tablespoons oil, the salt, flour mixture, and ½ cup water. On low speed, blend until the ingredients are combined, then remove the dough and knead it by hand for a couple minutes—it should be soft, but not sicky. Form a dough ball and place it in a bowl, cover, and let it rise at room temperature for 2 hours.

Preheat the oven to 350°F.

When the dough has doubled in volume, divide it into 8 small balls and roll each of these out to a 3-inch-diameter circle about ½ inch thick. Place them on a parchment-lined baking sheet and bake for 10 to 15 minutes until golden brown. Cool, and cut them open when you are ready to serve with your choice of charcuterie and cheeses.

LIMONCELLO GRANITA
with Whipped Cream

Limoncello, a sweet lemon liqueur, is popular across Italy and very easy to make and to find. I love to make homemade liqueurs with inspiration from the wide variety of fruit growing in our orchard, on our berry bushes, and in the rose garden. Limoncello is best kept ice-cold in the freezer, the way you might keep vodka. It's served here as a granita, with smooth whipped cream, a perfect pairing for a simple dessert.

Serves 6

½ cup sugar

½ cup limoncello

¼ cup fresh lemon juice

1 cup heavy cream, chilled

In a small saucepan, bring the sugar and 1 cup water to a simmer over medium heat. Cook for 1 to 2 minutes, just until the sugar dissolves and the liquid turns clear. Remove from the heat and let cool to room temperature. Stir in the limoncello and lemon juice.

Pour the mixture into a 9-inch-square glass or ceramic baking dish. Cover tightly with plastic wrap, and freeze for 45 minutes. Remove from the freezer and scrape the surface with a fork to break up the crystals, then cover and freeze for 1 hour.

Repeat this scraping/freezing process twice more, then cover and keep in the freezer until ready to serve, up to 2 weeks.

About 15 minutes before you are ready to serve, remove the granita from the freezer. In a wide bowl, using a handheld mixer or a whisk, whip the cream until thick and fluffy.

Just before serving, scrape the surface of the granita a final time. Serve in bowls topped with whipped cream.

LA FORTEZZA CHOCOLATE OLIVE OIL CAKE *with Rosemary Lemon Ice Cream*

This is a signature dessert at La Fortezza. We grow lemons and rosemary, and have an abundance of fresh olive oil in our region, so the ice cream is both delicious and locally sourced. Olive oil cakes can be dense, but this one uses only ½ cup olive oil, so it is light and delicate. The oil gives the cake a smooth finish and it holds up well the next day without being oily—I believe the cake lasts longer made with oil than with butter. You can substitute vanilla for the liqueur if you prefer. Note: The ice cream is a two-day process; I like to take the ice cream from the freezer about 15 minutes before serving, so it softens slightly and is easier to scoop. ✕ *Serves 8 to 10*

For the ice cream:

4 lemons

2 cups milk

1 cup heavy cream

½ cup sugar

2 tablespoons chopped fresh rosemary, divided

2 tablespoons cornstarch

½ teaspoon salt

For the cake:

½ cup extra virgin olive oil, plus 1 teaspoon for the pan

¼ cup cocoa powder, sifted

2 teaspoons China Clementi (or another bitter alcohol like Aperol, Fernet, or Amaretto)

½ teaspoon salt

1 cup all-purpose flour

1 teaspoon baking powder

1 ½ cups sugar

3 large eggs

To make the ice cream: Using a vegetable peeler, peel the lemons directly over a medium saucepan containing the milk and heavy cream—this way, fragrant oils are released by the peel falling into the pot. Set the pot over medium heat. Add the sugar and 1 tablespoon chopped rosemary, stirring constantly just until the sugar dissolves, then remove the pot from the heat.

Transfer 3 tablespoons of the warm mixture to a small bowl, and whisk in the cornstarch and salt to make a slurry. Add the cornstarch slurry back into the pot over low heat and whisk constantly for 2 minutes. Remove from the heat, stir in the rest of the rosemary, cover, and let it cool to room temperature before refrigerating overnight. The flavors need at least 8 hours to infuse.

The next day, pour the mixture through a fine-mesh strainer, discarding the lemon peel and rosemary. Transfer the infused mixture to an ice cream maker and freeze according to the manufacturer's instructions. Scrape the finished ice cream into a metal loaf pan, smooth the top, and cover tightly with plastic wrap. Keep in the freezer to set for at least 3 hours. This ice cream will keep in the freezer for up to 2 months.

To make the cake: Preheat the oven to 325°F.

Grease a 9-inch springform cake pan with 1 teaspoon oil, and cover the bottom with an ungreased parchment round.

In a small bowl, whisk ½ cup boiling water into the cocoa powder until smooth. Whisk in the China Clementi and salt, then set aside to cool.

In a separate bowl, whisk together the flour and baking powder.

In the bowl of a standing mixer fitted with the paddle attachment, combine the sugar, ½ cup olive oil, and the eggs and mix on medium-high speed for about 3 minutes until airy and thick. Reduce the speed to low and add the cocoa mixture. Stop the mixer to scrape down the sides and bottom of the bowl; then mix on low until evenly incorporated.

Slowly add the flour on low speed, about 1 minute, just until the batter comes together.

Pour the batter into the prepared pan, then tap it gently on the counter to remove any bubbles.

Bake for 40 to 45 minutes, until the sides of the cake pull away from the pan.

Remove and let cool about 1 hour, then remove the rim. Transfer the cake to a wire rack to cool completely.

Serve with the rosemary-lemon ice cream.

Autunno

AUTUMN
RECIPES

ROASTED GRAPE AND RICOTTA CROSTINI
with Salami

We had no idea when we bought the house that it came with a vineyard, but it was the perfect gift. Every September, right around my birthday, there is the grape harvest. One year our vintner, Manolo, left the most gorgeous arrangement of our grapes on the terrace table. It took my breath away. I made all sorts of things with them—12 pounds of grapes go a long way—including this aperitivo accompaniment. ✂ ***Serves 8 to 10***

1 pound red seedless grapes

½ cup plus 2 tablespoons extra virgin olive oil, divided

1 teaspoon salt, plus more for the ricotta

30 (1-inch) slices of rustic, hearty bread, cut into 3-inch pieces

1 ½ cups fresh ricotta

Freshly ground black pepper

30 thin slices hard salami

Preheat the oven to 350°F. Place the grapes on a baking sheet lined with parchment paper, and drizzle them with 2 tablespoons olive oil and 1 teaspoon salt. Roast for 30 minutes until they are softened but not dried and set aside to cool. The grapes will look plump and they deflate once they cool.

While the grapes roast, arrange the bread slices on two large rimmed baking sheets. Brush both sides with the remaining ½ cup oil. Bake for 15 to 20 minutes, rotating the sheets halfway through, until golden. Flip the crostini over once during baking. Let cool.

To assemble, spread the ricotta generously on each crostini and season with salt and pepper. Top each with a slice of salami and a small cluster of roasted grapes. Serve immediately.

Artisanal Vintner, Manolo Luchini

I had always dreamed of owning a vineyard, but never in my wildest dreams thought it would become a reality. We own about six acres of vines. You can imagine how thrilled we were to meet our vintner, Manolo, who worked the vineyard for the previous owners. Formerly a math teacher, he offered expertise that was more than welcome. It was a no-brainer as far as we were concerned to keep him and his family on, since we didn't know a thing about producing organic wine.

We quickly found out that we are part of a wine consortium, formed long before we arrived. What this means is that Manolo and his family work several vineyards, and produce wine that is sold to nearby restaurants and local wine vendors. We make a red (a pinot noir), and a lovely white (chardonnay), and a rosé.

Manolo started the business with his family—his father, Sergio, and his brother, Alessandro—twenty years ago. Their own family vineyard was planted in 1974. After making wine for family and friends from their vineyard, they decided to turn their passion into a business and started by replanting abandoned vineyards in the surrounding region. Some of the vineyards had been extremely neglected, but they discovered valuable vines that were vintage varieties. They felt it was very important to revive and regenerate these ancient varieties to add unique and authentic flavor profiles to the wine.

At La Fortezza, we discovered two such ancient vines on our grounds last year. We intend to start the process of grafting and replicating them to include in our vineyard with Manolo's help. All of our wine is certified organic, with no chemicals used and no added sulfites. Just the way I like it.

Manolo and his brother and father continue to expand all of the vineyards they work in. The family now produces fifteen thousand bottles per year. We use about one thousand bottles of wine annually, hosting and gifting wine to our guests. I use it in some of our dishes as well.

To quote Manolo: "The most beautiful part of our job is to live and work in this region, producing beautiful organic wines, with total respect for the environment that surrounds us. The biggest pleasure is sharing our production with our community."

PERSIMMON AND BRESAOLA ANTIPASTO

One of the things I have loved most about La Fortezza since the first time I saw it is the persimmon tree on the grounds. As it was summer, the tree was full of green orbs—back then I had no idea what they were. In the fall, we had an abundance of bright, soft, red-orange fruit. Our neighbors know a million ways to use them—drying, preserving, baking in cakes—but I prefer the fruit fresh. It has a sweet, smooth, silky taste. Moreover, it pairs well with my favorite salume, bresaola. This combination is magical. Use only the bright orange, ripe, soft persimmons; they are sour when green.

Serves 6

3 ripe persimmons, cut into wedges

8 ounces thinly sliced bresaola

2 tablespoons balsamic vinegar

2 tablespoons extra virgin olive oil

Wrap wedges of persimmon with bresaola and arrange on a platter. Drizzle with balsamic vinegar and olive oil. Serve immediately.

STUFFED PORCINI
with Parmesan and Breadcrumbs
(PORCINI RIPIENI)

Porcini mushrooms are harvested year-round in Italy. In America, they are mainly available in the fall. I get ours delivered from our mushroom-hunting neighbor, Cristian. He's our main supplier. Luckily, baby bella or cremini mushrooms are a great substitute. For fresh breadcrumbs, I like to blitz a slice of day-old bread in a food processor until crumbs form.

Serves 4 to 6

18 to 24 porcini mushrooms

2 tablespoons extra virgin olive oil

1 clove garlic, minced

2 tablespoons fresh breadcrumbs

2 tablespoons grated Parmesan cheese

1 large egg

1 teaspoon salt

½ teaspoon freshly ground black pepper

Preheat the oven to 375°F.

Clean the mushrooms and remove each stem to create a cavity; reserve and chop the stems to add to the stuffing. Toss the mushroom caps in the olive oil, then set aside.

To prepare the filling, combine garlic, chopped mushroom stems, breadcrumbs, Parmesan, egg, salt, and pepper in a bowl.

Stuff the mixture into the mushroom caps. Transfer to a baking sheet and bake for 10 to 12 minutes, until the cheese has melted and the mushrooms are soft. Serve at room temperature.

PRESERVED PORCINI MUSHROOMS

Porcini mushrooms are abundant in our region in the fall and spring. Our neighbors have so many they don't mind sharing with us. Everyone in the area is a master at preserving the bounty for the winter months. These preserved mushrooms are perfect to serve in the winter with a pork roast or in a risotto. If fresh porcini are not available, use cremini, portobello, or any such meaty mushroom. This is a quick preserving method, so the jars will need to be refrigerated; they will keep for up to 3 months. ✄ ***Yields two 1-pint (16-ounce) jars***

. . . .

3 pounds porcini mushrooms

¼ cup plus 2 tablespoons salt

4 cups white vinegar or cider vinegar

2 tablespoons dried oregano

Zest of 1 lemon, peeled in wide slices

2 cloves garlic, cut in half

6 dried hot chilies, split lengthwise

2 cups extra virgin olive oil, plus more as needed for filling the jars

. . . .

Slice the porcini mushrooms ½ inch thick. Toss the mushrooms with ¼ cup salt. Lay the mushrooms cut sides down on a baking sheet. Sprinkle another 2 tablespoons salt over the tops of all the mushrooms and let them brine for 2 hours at room temperature. Once they have released all of their moisture from the brining, pat and squeeze the mushrooms dry over the sink with a towel, being careful not to break them into pieces. They will release more water from the squeezing.

Transfer the brined mushrooms to a medium pot and add the vinegar. Bring to a boil over high heat, then reduce the heat to medium and cook for 5 minutes until soft. Drain and discard the vinegar.

Place the mushrooms on a parchment-lined baking sheet. Leave out at room temperature to dry for 18 to 24 hours.

Run the jars and their lids through a hot cycle on your dishwasher to sterilize.

In a large bowl, combine the dried mushrooms, oregano, lemon peel, garlic, and chilies, and toss until the mushrooms are thoroughly coated. Pack this mushroom mixture into the jars, distributing them evenly between the 2 jars. Carefully pour the oil into the jars to fill, making sure the mushrooms are fully submerged. Cover tightly with the lids and refrigerate for at least 1 week before serving.

SLOW-SMOKED PUMPKIN
with Toasted Hazelnuts and Pecorino

I make pizza all the time in our forno (outdoor pizza oven) at La Fortezza and I love building the fire. One great thing about the oven is that as the fire dies to a roasting temperature, I can cook several things at once. The oven holds the warmth for a good amount of time, and imparts a slightly smoked flavor. You can create the same effect at home using a smoker, like the Green Egg. Or you can use firewood in your grill to achieve a smoked effect. With this process you will need to mind the fire and keep adding firewood. Keep the grill covered to achieve the smoky flavor.

When you toast the hazelnuts, the skins will become blistered and loosen. You can either leave them on, or remove the skins easily with your hands once they have cooled, if you don't like the slightly bitter taste. Even though they are harvested in the fall, pumpkins will keep for months before you cook or bake them. Like watermelon, which we also smoke, pumpkins have a thick, hard rind that gives them a shelf life of 3 to 6 months; just keep them at room temperature in a cool, dark, dry place. This dish has become a regular on our Thanksgiving table. For best results with this recipe, use an outdoor fire source. This pumpkin blackens on the outside and is luscious and deliciously smoky and sweet on the inside.

Serves 6 to 8

1 cup hazelnuts

1 (4-pound) roasting pumpkin (a Cinderella variety works well)

2 tablespoons extra virgin olive, plus ¼ cup for oiling the pumpkin

1 teaspoon salt

¼ cup shredded pecorino cheese

Heat a grill, smoker, Green Egg, or forno to 300°F. Preheat the oven to 375°F.

Toast the hazelnuts in the oven for 5 minutes. Watch carefully so they do not burn. Let them cool, rub off the skins if desired, then chop into pieces and set aside.

Oil the pumpkin on all sides with ¼ cup oil. Place directly on the grill, or in a cast-iron skillet if using a forno, and roast on low heat for at least 3 to 4 hours, until it is blackened and has almost collapsed. Note: You may need to add logs to the fire to keep the temperature at 300°F throughout the process.

Cut the pumpkin in half, scoop out and discard the seeds, and scrape the flesh into a food processor fitted with a metal blade. Add the salt and the remaining 2 tablespoons oil and pulse until smooth.

Transfer the pumpkin puree to a serving bowl and top with shredded pecorino and toasted hazelnuts. Serve warm.

ROASTED CAULIFLOWER
with Spicy Anchovy Garlic Sauce
(CAVOLFIORI CON L'ACCIUGATA)

This dish embodies every sour, sweet, salty, and spicy flavor that I love. Caramelizing the cauliflower seals in the sweetness of this popular vegetable. To avoid using the oven, simply toss the cauliflower in 3 tablespoons olive oil and sauté it over medium-low heat for 12 to 15 minutes, stirring several times, until it browns overall.

Serves 4

1 head cauliflower, trimmed and cut into florets

¼ cup plus 3 tablespoons extra virgin olive oil, divided

1 teaspoon salt

2 cloves garlic, crushed

3 teaspoons anchovy paste

¼ cup capers, rinsed and drained

½ teaspoon red pepper flakes

2 tablespoons lemon juice (about ½ lemon)

Preheat the oven to 400°F.

Toss the cauliflower florets in ¼ cup olive oil, season with salt, and transfer to a roasting pan. Roast for 30 to 40 minutes until fork tender. Place in a serving bowl and keep warm.

In a sauté pan over low heat, warm the remaining 3 tablespoons olive oil and sauté the garlic for 3 to 5 minutes, or until slightly browned. Whisk in the anchovy paste, capers, and red pepper flakes and remove from the heat. Spoon the oil and capers over the cauliflower. Drizzle with lemon juice and serve warm.

CANNELLINI BEANS IN A FLASK
(FAGIOLI NEL FIASCO)

Most old homes in Italy have a fireplace in the kitchen, and it became the central heat in a house back in the day. In the winter families would congregate in the kitchen and use the fireplace for both heating and cooking. Tuscan farmers cooked beans on the embers of the fireplace where most meals were cooked. They would place the beans with water and spices in a glass jar—most likely a chianti bottle—in a corner of the fireplace on the embers before going to bed. The next morning the beans would be cooked and warm. I use La Fortezza's traditional outdoor forno (pizza oven) to cook beans in this manner. The slow cooking results in creamier beans, but you can replicate this easily in the oven. I've included a way to use the flask if you want to try the ancient way. Just make sure that the glass is ovenproof; I like to use canning jars. You will need two 1-quart jars for this recipe. **Makes two 1-quart jars**

....

2 cups dried cannellini beans

¼ cup plus 2 tablespoons extra virgin olive oil

4 cloves garlic, crushed

12 sage leaves

1 teaspoon salt

½ teaspoon freshly ground black pepper

....

To prepare in a flask: Soak the beans in 8 cups water overnight, or for at least 8 hours.

Preheat the oven to 250°F.

Divide the soaked beans evenly between the two 1-quart jars; add enough water to fill the jars, leaving 2 inches headspace at the top. Add 2 crushed garlic cloves, 6 sage leaves, ½ teaspoon salt and ¼ teaspoon black pepper to each jar. Cover the jars loosely with the lids to make sure that the steam can escape. Fill the pot three-quarters full with water, set the filled jars into the water, and bake in the oven for 3 to 4 hours until the beans look creamy and are fork soft. You can leave them in the oven for as long as 6 hours; they will only get creamier.

I like to bring the warm jars to the table and serve everyone directly from them.

To prepare in a Dutch oven: Soak the beans in 8 cups water overnight, or for at least 8 hours.

The next day, preheat the oven to 250°F.

Drain the beans and place them in a large Dutch oven. Add the oil, garlic, and sage leaves and cover with 6 cups water. Cook in the lower portion of the oven for 3 to 4 hours until the beans are soft and creamy.

BUTTERNUT SQUASH AND POTATO PIE
(TORTA DI ZUCCA E PATATE)

I prepare a lot of squash from the garden. This pie is filling—and inexpensive to prepare. The buttery flavor is rich and satisfying, and this pie tastes great, warm or cold, and it serves as a main dish for vegetarian meals.

⅏ *Serves 8*

For the quick puff pastry
(or 1 disk store-bought puff pastry):
2 cups all-purpose flour, plus more
for work surface
1 teaspoon salt
2 ½ sticks frozen unsalted butter

For the filling:
1 pound potatoes, peeled and cut into 2-inch
cubes (about 2 ½ cups)
1 teaspoon salt, divided
1 ¼ cups grated Parmesan cheese, divided
3 tablespoons extra virgin olive oil
1 pound butternut squash, peeled and
cut into 2-inch cubes (about 2 ½ cups)
2 cloves garlic, minced
1 large egg, beaten
½ teaspoon freshly grated nutmeg
2 tablespoons unsalted butter, melted

Prepare the puff pastry up to one day ahead. Place 2 cups flour and the salt in the bowl of a standing mixer fitted with a paddle attachment. Use a vegetable grater to grate the frozen butter into the flour. On slow speed, add ½ cup cold water until a thick dough forms; then gather the dough into a ball, flatten it into a 4 by 5-inch rectangle, and wrap in plastic wrap. Refrigerate for 1 hour or place it in the freezer for 20 to 30 minutes.

Unwrap the chilled dough; dust your work surface with flour and roll out the dough into a 6 by 12-inch rectangle. Fold the dough in thirds, like a letter. Turn it 90 degrees, roll out the dough to a 6 by 12-inch rectangle and fold into thirds again. Repeat this process 2 to 4 times; then wrap the dough in plastic wrap and refrigerate for at least 2 hours or overnight.

Remove the puff pastry from the refrigerator about 15 minutes before using, to soften.

To make the filling: Place the potatoes in a pot with enough cold water to cover, bring to a simmer over medium heat, and cook for 20 minutes, or until the potatoes are soft. Drain well, and toss with ½ teaspoon salt and 1 cup Parmesan cheese. Set aside in a large bowl.

Heat the oil in a sauté pan over medium heat and sauté the squash, garlic, and remaining ½ teaspoon salt for 15 minutes, or until the squash is soft.

Preheat the oven to 350°F.

Gently toss the cooked squash in a bowl with the potatoes, being careful not to break up the squash, then stir in the egg, nutmeg, and butter. Set aside.

Roll out the puff pastry and press it into an 8-inch springform pan. Using your fingers or a fork, press the pastry around the rim of the pan and use a fork to prick the bottom.

Place the potato and squash filling into the puff pastry and smooth the top with a spatula. Bake for 25 minutes, then top with the remaining ¼ cup Parmesan cheese and continue to bake for 10 minutes, or until the pastry is golden brown.

Serve warm or at room temperature.

STUFFED ONIONS
with Mortadella and Greens

As you can tell, stuffing vegetables is popular in the Tuscan countryside. It is a great way to make vegetables into a complete meal. One thing about this recipe you will notice is the addition of mortadella. What the Lunigianesi refer to as mortadella is not the same meat we think of in the United States. In Lunigiana, mortadella is a sweet, soft salami similar to the Genoa salami we have in the States. You can make this dish with any soft Italian salami, if you can't find this regional version. ✗ *Serves 4*

4 medium red onions

1 ½ cups finely chopped chard

½ cup finely chopped mortadella (about 8 ounces), or other soft salami

¼ cup shredded Parmesan cheese

4 large eggs

1 teaspoon salt

¼ cup plus 2 tablespoons extra virgin olive oil

1 cup vegetable broth

Preheat the oven to 375°F.

Peel and cut the tops off the onions, ¾-inch from the very top, and cut off the bottom of each onion so it sits flat. Gently remove the core and inside layers of the onion with a paring knife, so that the onion is hollow, but still rigid enough to hold the stuffing. Chop enough of the removed onion to yield ½ cup.

In a large bowl, combine the chopped chard, mortadella, chopped onion, Parmesan, eggs, and salt and mix thoroughly.

Spoon the mixture into the cavities of the cored onions, filling them to the top. Transfer to a 2-quart roasting pan. Drizzle with the oil, add the broth, and bake for 25 minutes until fork tender. Serve warm.

TESTAROLI

A signature dish of Lunigiana, often described as "the earliest recorded pasta," testaroli originated in the ancient Etruscan civilization. It is similar to a crepe, prepared in a special iron skillet called a testo. *The testo is traditionally a flat cast-iron cooking surface. The crepe is then cut into diamond shapes, and sometimes cooked further in boiling water. When you order testaroli in a restaurant, you are asked to choose how you want it dressed: with pesto, ragù, or other ingredients, such as olive oil, topped with grated pecorino or Parmesan cheese.*

Serves 4 to 6

1 cup 00 flour

1 tablespoon salt

1 teaspoon baking powder

3 tablespoons extra virgin olive oil

½ cup pesto (recipe, page 27)

⅓ cup grated Parmesan cheese

Preheat the oven to 450°F.

Mix the flour, salt, and baking powder in a bowl, and stir in 2 ½ cups water and the oil.

Place a cast-iron skillet into the oven. Once the skillet is hot (it takes about 2 minutes to heat), remove with an oven mitt and ladle in 1 cup of the batter. Set the skillet with the batter over medium heat on the cooktop, and when the top of the testaroli is pale and filled with holes, flip it, cook another 20 seconds, and use a spatula to remove it from the pan and place on a cutting board. Repeat with the remaining batter.

Cut the testaroli into 2-inch diamonds and blanch them in a pot of boiling water for 30 seconds, then drain on paper towels.

When the testaroli have dried, spoon a dollop of pesto on each diamond and sprinkle with Parmesan. Serve as appetizers or with aperitivo.

Testaroli Master of Pontremoli, Fabrizio Botta

When I first moved to Lunigiana, I was introduced to the medieval food called testaroli, known as the ancient pasta of Italy. I was intrigued to see how it was made, and my friend Giovanna took me to meet the testaroli master, Fabrizio. When we met he shook my hand with his smoke-blackened one and lead me into his fiery workshop. Heavy cast-iron pans known as testi were lined up on a long fire pit, a pulley system in place to hoist the incredibly heavy lids (one testo may weigh sixty pounds) so he could pull the finished crepes from the pans. As he fed the fire, I imagined that the cooking technique had not changed much since medieval times. Like an ancient production line, Fabrizio worked non-stop making the giant crepes.

He cut one of the crepes into diamonds, doused it in his family's olive oil, and offered it to me. The soft, nutty taste and crispy texture is so simple, yet divine, and I understood why this local dish is still popular to this day. I said, "Buono," and Fabrizio smiled, his rugged, lined face smeared with soot. This is his passion and his calling, to preserve this ancient recipe and technique. All the folks who uphold these traditions are the reason I love this region so much, and why testaroli, the ancient pasta of Lunigiana, is here to stay.

CHESTNUT RAVIOLI
with Chard and Ricotta
(RAVIOLI DI CASTAGNE CON RIPIENO DI VERDURA)

Chestnut flour gives the ravioli a smoky, nutty flavor. The sage adds a fragrant, earthy note that brings back memories—the smell of cooked stuffing in the Thanksgiving turkey, and the burnt olive branches after the harvest in November. This dish embodies fall in Lunigiana—not only what we grow, but how we eat. This recipe calls for pecorino salata, a sheep's milk ricotta that is dried, salted, and pressed. It has a mild, sweet, nutty flavor and is excellent for grating. You can use other pecorino cheese as well. You must be careful not to burn the butter—it should be the color of maple syrup. ✻ *Serves 4 to 6*

Chestnut Pasta dough (recipe, page 35)

3 tablespoons extra virgin olive oil, plus 3 tablespoons for serving

5 cups stemmed and chopped loosely packed chard or beet greens

½ teaspoon salt, plus ¼ cup for cooking the pasta

2 tablespoons dry white wine

2 cups ricotta

1 cup grated pecorino salata or pecorino romano, divided

1 large egg, beaten

1 stick (8 tablespoons) unsalted butter

¼ cup chopped fresh sage

½ teaspoon freshly ground black pepper

Prepare the chestnut pasta dough according to instructions.

To make the filling, heat 3 tablespoons olive oil in a large skillet over medium-high heat; add the chard and ½ teaspoon salt and cook for 5 minutes, stirring frequently, until the greens soften and wilt. Pour in the wine and 2 tablespoons water and continue cooking for about 5 minutes, until the greens are tender and the liquid is fully reduced. Set aside to cool.

Once the chard has cooled, transfer it to a bowl and mix in the ricotta and ½ cup grated pecorino and the beaten egg.

Place the filling into a piping bag fitted with a number 8 or 9 (large) tip.

To prepare the ravioli, roll out the pasta dough as thinly as possible into a large circle at least 22 inches in diameter and ⅛ inch thick. Using a sharp knife and a ruler, trim and cut the dough into seven strips; the finished strips should be about 3 inches wide by 20 inches long. Starting about 1 inch from the end, pipe 1 scant teaspoon of the filling onto a strip of dough, about ¾ inch from a side edge.

Continue to pipe balls of filling every 2 ½ inches down the strip. Use a pastry brush dipped in water to moisten the edges around the filling.

Fold the dough over the filling to cover. Use your fingers to press the dough tightly around the filling to seal, pushing out any air bubbles. Using a pasta wheel, trim the ravioli on all four sides to form 1 by 2-inch rectangles. Repeat with the remaining strips of dough and filling.

To prepare the sauce, melt the butter in a skillet over medium heat, and cook for about 3 to 5 minutes until it turns a caramel color. Make sure the butter does not burn. Stir in the sage and remove from heat.

Bring a large pot of water to a boil over medium-high heat, salt it with the remaining ¼ cup salt, add the ravioli, and stir immediately so they do not stick together. Cook for 1 ½ to 2 minutes, until the pasta floats to the top and is al dente.

Using a spider strainer or slotted spoon, remove the pasta to a large serving bowl, toss with the browned sage butter, top with black pepper and the remaining ½ cup pecorino, and serve warm.

TAGLIATELLE
with Salt Cod in Tomato Sauce
(TAGLIATELLE CON LA BACCALÀ AL SUGO DI POMODORO)

This is a typical fisherman's lunch, served often on the nearby coast. It's simple and quick to prepare, and I often see diners enjoying this around the fishermen's cove in Portovenere. It's the perfect dish to highlight all the tomatoes that were jarred and put up in the summer.

Serves 4

4 cups baccalà (salted cod), broken into bite-size pieces
Basic Egg Pasta Dough (recipe, page 30)
3 tablespoons extra virgin olive oil
1 small onion, chopped
4 (14-ounce) cans Mutti Polpa chopped tomatoes, or another good-quality brand

2 cloves garlic, minced
½ teaspoon salt, plus ¼ cup for cooking the pasta
½ teaspoon freshly ground black pepper
2 tablespoons hot pepper oil
2 tablespoons dried thyme leaves

In a large bowl, cover the fish with approximately 2 inches of cold water. Cover the bowl, refrigerate, and allow the fish to soak for up to 3 days (similar to soaking a ham to rid it of excess salt), changing the water at least twice each day. This method softens the cod and removes the excess salt it has been preserved in, so it is soft and flaky when cooked. After 3 days remove from the water and let dry on paper towels.

When you are ready to cook, make the pasta dough, roll it out, and cut it into ¼-inch-wide tagliatelle noodles.

Heat the oil in a large saucepan over medium heat and sauté the onion in the oil for 3 to 5 minutes, until tender. Add the tomatoes and garlic and simmer for 20 minutes. Add the cod pieces to the tomato sauce and season with ½ teaspoon salt and pepper. Simmer for 10 minutes, until the cod is cooked through but not so soft it falls apart in the sauce.

Meanwhile, bring a large pot of water to a boil, salt it with the remaining ¼ cup salt, add the tagliatelle, and cook until al dente, about 5 minutes. Remove with a spider strainer and toss the pasta into the pan with the sauce. Sprinkle with hot pepper oil and dried thyme leaves, transfer to bowls, and serve warm.

PAPPARDELLE WITH DUCK RAGÙ

A forest extends into our land and, in Italy, I discovered that hunters can legally hunt on anyone's property. One morning very soon after we moved into La Fortezza, I wandered into the garden with my espresso and noticed about ten trucks and SUVs parked in the backyard. Lots of guys dressed in olive drab, holding guns, were standing around talking while hunting dogs ran around barking. I quickly called a friend, who explained the laws to me. They can only hunt on certain days, so on Wednesdays they hunt birds—anything that flies. On weekends they can hunt boar. At first I waved and smiled and they seemed startled to see me. Now they hunt regularly on my property in the fall, and then drop off a duck or pheasant or a boar for us, as a gift. Once I got over the shock, it's become a harmonious relationship—except for the ducks! This ragù can be made a day ahead. ✄ **Serves 4**

2 tablespoons extra virgin olive oil

4 (1-pound) duck legs

1 teaspoon salt, plus ¼ cup for cooking the pasta

½ teaspoon freshly ground black pepper

1 small yellow onion, chopped

1 large carrot, chopped

2 stalks celery, chopped

4 ounces cubed speck, or 3 slices bacon, diced

2 tablespoons chopped fresh rosemary

1 teaspoon dried oregano

1 cup red wine

3 cloves garlic, minced

1 cup beef stock

Basic Egg Pasta Dough (recipe, page 30)

½ cup grated Parmesan cheese, for serving

Preheat the oven to 350°F.

In a 3-quart Dutch oven over medium, heat the oil until shimmering.

Season the duck legs with 1 teaspoon salt and pepper. Add them to the Dutch oven and cook until browned on both sides, about 10 minutes. Remove and set aside. Pour off all but 2 tablespoons of fat from the pot. Add the onion, carrot, celery, speck, rosemary, and oregano and cook on medium heat until the vegetables are soft and the onions are translucent, about 10 minutes. Deglaze with the wine, scraping all the browned bits from the bottom of the pot, and cook until the liquid is slightly reduced, about 3 to 5 minutes. Add the garlic, seared duck legs, and stock. Cover and bake for 1 hour 30 minutes.

While the meat is roasting, make the pasta dough, roll it out, and cut it into ½-inch-wide pappardelle noodles.

Remove the duck legs from the Dutch oven. Let them cool enough to handle, then use a fork to pull the meat off the bone and shred (you can also use your hands to shred; this is my preferred method). Return the duck meat to the sauce and place on the cooktop over low heat to keep warm.

Bring a large pot of water to a boil, salt it with the remaining ¼ cup salt, add the pappardelle, and cook until al dente, about 5 minutes. Remove with a spider strainer. Place the pasta on a large platter and serve topped with the ragù and Parmesan.

WHOLE GRILLED TURBOT
with Pickled Vegetables and Polenta

Drawing on things from the pantry that I preserved from the summer garden, I can extend the peak flavors of the season into the fall. This grilled fish pairs well with sweet pickled zucchini, peppers, and eggplant (recipe, page 70). Serve with a side of polenta, the perfect starch to counterbalance the bold flavors of this dish.
Turbot, rombo *in Italian, is a fish commonly found at fish markets in the autumn in Lunigiana. Known for its fatty and flaky consistency, it's easy to grill. The sour notes from the pickled vegetables make this dish a showstopper.*

Serves 8 to 10

2 tablespoons salt

2 cups white wine

10 whole black peppercorns

1 (3-pound) turbot

Polenta for serving 8 to 10 (recipe, page 42)

Pickled Zucchini, Peppers, and Eggplant (recipe, page 70)

Combine the salt, wine, and peppercorns to make a brine, and pour it over the fish in a container large enough so that the brine covers the fish. Cover and refrigerate for at least 6 hours, or overnight.

When you are ready to cook, prepare the grill.

While the grill heats up, make the polenta.

To grill the fish, place the fish dark side down (note that turbot has a dark and light side), then grill for 10 minutes, turn, and grill for another 10 minutes, until the meat is flaky.

Pour the polenta out onto a large platter, top with the grilled turbot, and serve with the pickled vegetables (plan to make these 1 week ahead).

BRAISED CHICKEN AND PORCINI
with Chestnut Polenta
(POLLO E POCCIA DI PORCINI, CON POLENTA DI CASTAGNA)

The locals raise chickens in their backyards. They don't eat chicken very often, because the eggs are more valuable to them than the meat, but most likely in the fall they will sacrifice one of them to make this tasty dish. Since it's autumn, the chestnuts are milled and smoked and ground into flour. The first milled chestnut flour is available at this time, and this dish celebrates that occasion. You can use rehydrated dried porcini mushrooms in place of fresh, along with their soaking liquid. ✂ *Serves 4*

For the chicken:

1 (2-pound) bone-in chicken, cut in 4 to 6 pieces

1 cup all-purpose flour

3 tablespoons extra virgin olive oil

1 stalk celery, diced

1 small onion, diced

1 carrot, diced

1 tablespoon chopped fresh rosemary

1 tablespoon chopped fresh sage

½ teaspoon salt

¼ teaspoon freshly ground pepper

1 cup red wine

1 cup beef broth

1 pound (4 cups) sliced fresh porcini mushrooms, or 5 ounces dried porcini rehydrated in 1 cup warm water to yield 4 cups

(Note: If rehydrating the mushrooms you can use the rehydrating water in place of the beef broth.)

For the chestnut polenta:

1 teaspoon salt

4 cups chestnut flour

To make the chicken: Preheat the oven to 350°F.

Dry the chicken pieces and dredge them in the flour. Shake to remove any excess.

Heat the oil in a Dutch oven over medium heat, and sear the chicken pieces in batches until browned, 3 to 5 minutes on each side. Remove them from the pot and set aside.

In the same pot, sauté the celery, onion, and carrot over medium heat for 3 to 5 minutes until transparent and soft. Add the rosemary, sage, salt, pepper, wine, and beef broth (or porcini soaking liquid), and return the chicken to the pot. Cover and bake for 2 hours, or until fork tender and fragrant.

To make the polenta: In a large pot, bring 4 cups water and the salt to a boil over medium-high heat. Slowly whisk the chestnut flour into the pot in a steady stream. With a spoon, stir for approximately 10 minutes, until you have a creamy texture. The polenta will thicken and bubble, and will have a porridge-like consistency. If there are any lumps, break them up and continue to stir until creamy.

To serve, place a dollop of polenta on each plate and top with the chicken and mushroom sauce. Serve immediately.

HERBED PORK, CRANBERRY BEANS, AND GREENS *with Fried Polenta*

I grew up on pig's feet—Hungarians love them. Some cultures use every piece of the pig, and the Italian way of using the entire product is especially important in the countryside. Pork trotters, or pig's feet, as they are commonly known, are the traditional ingredients in this recipe, but they're not something most people are familiar with. With this in mind I have amended the recipe using pork loin. If you are a fan of pig's feet, of course you can use trotters, just make sure they have been cleaned properly, and add an additional ½ cup water when roasting. This is a homey dish, incorporating the cranberry beans that are so popular in Lunigiana. I recommend fresh beans for this recipe, but you can easily use dried.
Note: The polenta must sit overnight before frying. 🌿 ***Serves 4 to 6***

....

Polenta (recipe, page 42)

2 cups fresh or dried cranberry beans

2 tablespoons fresh rosemary

3 fresh sage leaves

5 cloves garlic, 3 whole, 2 minced

½ cup plus 1 tablespoon extra virgin olive oil, divided

3 tablespoons Dijon mustard

2 tablespoons plus 1 teaspoon salt, divided

1 (4 to 4 ½-pound) boneless pork loin roast, trimmed

6 bunches of kale

1 small yellow onion, chopped

1 (14-ounce) can Mutti Polpa chopped tomatoes, or 1 ¾ cups La Fortezza Tomato Sauce (recipe, page 76)

1 teaspoon freshly ground black pepper

....

Make the polenta the day before you plan to fry it. Pour it into a 4-quart rimmed casserole dish. Cover with plastic wrap and refrigerate overnight.

Wash the cranberry beans and set aside. If using dried beans, soak them in 4 cups water overnight, or for at least 8 hours, rinse, then simmer in enough water to cover for 1 to 2 hours until soft.

Preheat the oven to 350°F. Place the rack in the middle.

In the bowl of a food processor fitted with the metal blade, combine the rosemary, sage, 3 whole garlic cloves, 2 tablespoons olive oil, the mustard, and 2 tablespoons salt. Pulse until a chunky paste forms. Pat the pork dry, and rub it all over with the paste.

Place the pork into a roasting pan, add ½ cup water, and roast for 1 hour, or until an instant-read thermometer registers 140 to 145°F (the temperature will rise 5 to 10°F as it rests). Transfer to a cutting board and let it rest for 15 to 25 minutes.

Clean the kale by stripping the leaves from the thick stems. Strip the leaf by gripping the bottom of the stem in one hand, then pinching the leaf with your thumb and index finger on either side, and run your fingers up the stem to separate the leaf from the stem. Roll the leaves and cut into thin strips; you will need 6 cups loosely packed kale strips.

Add 3 tablespoons olive oil and the onion to a large skillet over medium heat and cook for 3 to 5 minutes, until the onion is translucent. Reduce the heat to low and add the beans and cook for 10 minutes until warmed through, then add the kale, tomatoes, minced garlic, 1 teaspoon each salt and pepper, and ½ cup water. Cover the pan and cook for 10 minutes, stirring occasionally, until the kale has wilted and cooked down.

While the beans cook, cut the chilled polenta into 3-inch squares.

Place the remaining ¼ cup olive oil in a large non-stick skillet over medium heat and fry the polenta slices in batches, being careful not to overcrowd the pan, about 3 to 5 minutes per side, until golden brown and crisp. Remove with a slotted spatula and place on paper towels to drain. Add additional oil if needed.

To serve, place the fried polenta squares on a platter, top with sliced pork and the beans and kale. Serve warm.

Butcher, Modesto Bertocchi

Teri, one of our first workshop chefs, and I wandered into a small butcher shop on the main street of our tiny village of Fivizzano one day. We both smiled as soon as we crossed the threshold of this local shop, because it was the quintessential Italian butcher shop, with beautifully displayed cuts of meat in the display case all lit with a pink light to showcase the meat.

Behind the counter the entire family stood ready to take our order. Modesto, the butcher, greeted us, and behind him were two women—his wife and daughter. You could tell by the way they wielded a cleaver that they had been working in the shop for many years. We quickly learned that Modesto opened this butcher shop twenty-five years earlier under the guidance of his father, who had a butcher shop during World War II

in Sassalbo, a small mountain village. Modesto specializes in the processing of salami that he sells throughout Lunigiana.

I have been patronizing his shop since that first visit. Not only do I love his bistecca (recipe, page 82), but his porchetta, a stuffed pork roll made with fatback and stuffed with a variety of herbs and garlic, is fantastic. I usually make porchetta myself, but one day we were running behind preparing a dinner party and I needed something quickly. I ordered his porchetta, and it was a genius decision! I picked it up at the shop around six o'clock and served it at room temperature with roasted potatoes (recipe, page 160). I am excited to share his recipe on the following page.

MODESTO'S PORCHETTA

Modesto was excited to share this recipe but shy about giving it to me, so I asked my friend Federica, whose farmacia (pharmacy) is next door to his shop and who knows him well, to ask him questions about how he made it. The most important thing is that the pork belly is trimmed properly, about ¾ inch thick, so it will roll easily and cook more evenly. Dried juniper berries add a bright freshness—they are somewhat like peppercorns.
Porchetta leftovers make fantastic sandwiches on warm focaccia.

Serves 10

1 (5- to 6-pound) fresh pork belly, trimmed into a
12 by 18-inch rectangle
1 (2 to 3-pound) boneless, center cut pork loin
3 cloves garlic
1 tablespoon fresh rosemary leaves
2 tablespoons chopped fresh sage
1 fresh bay leaf

1 teaspoon dried juniper berries
1 tablespoon salt, divided
1 teaspoon freshly ground black pepper
¼ cup extra virgin olive oil
Juice of 1 lemon

Set the pork belly skin side down on a clean work surface. Using a knife, score the flesh in a checkerboard pattern, ⅓ inch deep. This step ensures the roast will cook evenly. Flip the pork skin side up and, with a sharp paring knife, poke shallow holes through the skin, all over the belly. Pound the pork loin to a ½- to ¾-inch thickness.

In a food processor fitted with a metal blade, pulse together the garlic, rosemary, sage, bay leaf, juniper berries, 1 teaspoon salt, the pepper, olive oil, and lemon juice until the herb mixture forms a paste.

Using the jagged edge of a meat mallet, pound the belly skin all over for 3 minutes to tenderize it; this will help crisp the skin when roasted. Flip over and season the belly and the flattened loin with the remaining 2 teaspoons salt. Place the loin lengthwise down the center of the checkerboard side of the belly. Spread the herb paste evenly on top of the loin.

To form the porchetta log, start at the short end, and use both hands to roll the belly and loin away from you around the herb paste to form a log.

Secure the roll tightly with kitchen twine in at least 4 places. Wrap in plastic and refrigerate for 24 hours.

About 2 hours before roasting, take the porchetta out of the refrigerator and remove the plastic wrap. Let it sit on the counter to come to room temperature.

Preheat the oven to 500°F.

Place the porchetta on a rack in a roasting pan and roast for 40 minutes. After 40 minutes, reduce the heat to 325°F and continue roasting for 2 hours, until an instant-read thermometer inserted into the center of the meat reads 145°F. Rotate the pan and turn the porchetta occasionally to cook evenly. If the skin is not a deep brown color and crispy after this time, return the oven to 500°F and roast it for an additional 10 minutes.

Let the porchetta rest at room temperature for 30 minutes. Remove the twine and, using a serrated knife, cut it into ½-inch-thick slices. Serve warm or at room temperature.

Truffle Hunter, Simone Mori and His Dog, Tito

I met my friend Simone, a truffle hunter, and his dog Tito a few years ago. Tito the truffle dog is a breed called Lagotto Romagnolo; in Tuscany this is the dominant dog breed for hunting truffles.

It's a funny story, and pretty typical of the way I operate. As research for this book, I arranged a truffle excursion through my friend Cornelia (see page 138). We met at her place and she drove me to the industrial part of Pontremoli; and there on the side of the road sat Simone in his beat up SUV, waiting to take me into the forest. I waved goodbye to Cornelia and hopped into the car, alone with a man I had never met, to drive into the woods.

Once we drove away it occurred to me that maybe I had not thought this through. Was this crazy? What had I been thinking? But as with most things, I just went for it, so I settled in. Lucky for me Simone was a friendly, chatty guy. He spoke perfect English and shared the history of how he became a truffle hunter. We drove for about forty-five minutes into the mountains, while Simone explained the terrain and why the forest floor held these delicious treasures. I could tell he was passionate about foraging mushrooms and truffles—and also treasures. He was an avid relic hunter, and loved to hike through the countryside with his metal detector.

Simone explained that his father was a famous mushroom forager, and had begun to teach Simone how to forage at the age of four. He went on to study with a truffle hunter who was in his nineties, and that teacher had shared all his special hunting places and secrets.

When we got out of the car, Simone handed me a walking stick and told me I would need it. I was not sure I believed him, but I took it anyway (he was right—walking through the woods was treacherous). I watched him walk to the back of the car, where there was a crate, and in the crate was his truffle dog, Tito. I could tell this dog was very special. He smiled at us, and jumped out of the car and headed straight into the forest. We followed along, and in about three minutes he was already digging in the ground and had found a truffle, the first one I had ever seen fresh from the earth. That was it for me—I was hooked. We hunted for about three more hours. It was one of the best experiences of my life, which goes to show you that sometimes you just have to take a chance.

Simone and I are good friends now and we love to organize hunting trips for my workshops and guests, and they love it too. Tito is still the most amazing dog I have ever met. The truffles he finds are incredible. Simone hunts all year—and yes, you can hunt truffles in the summer. In fact, there are nine types that grow in our region. The most flavorful—the black and white truffles—are found in the fall. After our organized excursions, we always end with lunch at Podere Conti; however, Simone likes his truffles in the Italian tradition, shaved atop an over-easy fried egg. Tito likes his right out of the terra.

PODERE CONTI TRUFFLE AND CHESTNUT-STUFFED RABBIT
with Pecorino Cream and Radicchio

Serves 4 to 6

20 boiled chestnuts (see Source Guide, page 205)

1 tablespoon grated fresh truffle, plus slices for serving (see Source Guide, page 205)

7 tablespoons unsalted butter, softened, divided

2 tablespoons all-purpose flour

½ cup milk

1 cup grated pecorino romano cheese

2 tablespoons thinly sliced sage leaves

2 (1½-pound) rabbits, deboned

1 teaspoon salt

1 teaspoon freshly ground black pepper

15 to 20 thin slices of pancetta, guanciale, or bacon

3 tablespoons extra virgin olive oil

For the radicchio:

2 tablespoons extra virgin olive oil

1 cup red wine vinegar

1 teaspoon sugar

1 teaspoon salt

½ teaspoon freshly ground black pepper

4 small heads radicchio (2 ounces each)

Preheat the oven to 350°F.

In the bowl of a food processor fitted with a metal blade, combine the chestnuts, grated truffle, and 3 tablespoons butter. Process until the mixture forms a rough paste, about 10 seconds.

To prepare the pecorino cream, melt the remaining 4 tablespoons butter in a small saucepan over medium heat. Add the flour then slowly add the milk to form a béchamel sauce. Add the pecorino, stirring until the sauce comes together, about 2 minutes. It should coat the spoon. Add the sage leaves and set aside to steep for 30 minutes to infuse with the sage.

Lay one deboned rabbit cavity side up on a clean work space. Season with salt and pepper, and layer half the pancetta slices slightly overlapping to cover the majority of the cavity. Spread half the chestnut truffle paste over the pancetta, leaving a ¼-inch border around the edge. Roll the rabbit lengthwise, tuck in the ends, and tie generously with kitchen twine into one roll about 7 inches long. Repeat with the other rabbit.

Heat the olive oil in a large frying pan over medium-high heat and sear the outside of the rabbits until brown, about 5 minutes. Transfer them to a Dutch oven, cover, and bake for 30 minutes. Remove from the oven and let rest for 10 minutes before slicing.

While the rabbit rests, prepare the radicchio: In a cast-iron skillet over medium heat, add the oil, vinegar, sugar, salt, and pepper; add the radicchio and sauté for about 10 minutes until it is wilted but still maintains its shape.

Cut the rabbit into 1-inch-diameter medallions and remove any kitchen twine. Serve with generous drizzles of warmed pecorino cream, truffle slices, some of the rabbit jus, and the radicchio on the side.

Agriturismo Podere Conti Owner and Olive Oil Producer, Cornelia Conti

Cornelia and I first connected on the Internet. I was searching for a truffle excursion, and her site was the first to come up. We set a time and met in person, and we quickly realized we had a lot in common, including our matching vintage Range Rovers.

Cornelia is a strong, independent woman on a mission. Her vision has always been self-sufficiency and sustainability. Agriturismo Podere Conti is her working farm. The farm is certified organic, and they implement alternative energy and rainwater collection for agricultural use. They produce and sell the most divine olive oil; they raise lambs to eat, and use the vegetables from their massive kitchen garden to supply their restaurant that specializes in local dishes. Guests stay on the expansive grounds and enjoy bucolic views of the sheep in the pasture and the acres of olive groves.

The bed-and-breakfast can hold forty-two guests, and the restaurant can seat one hundred. Cornelia started hosting weddings there, because it's the perfect venue for rustic chic weddings in the middle of the countryside.

When the property was purchased in 2003, it included three stone ruins and 200 acres. It took three years to complete the purchase; planning took one year; and the restoration started in 2006. Four years later, in 2010, the doors were opened to the public. The main building was deconstructed and rebuilt using the original stones and beams, essentially a new structure recycling all the old materials. Cornelia was very deliberate about keeping the original footprint of the building. As she told me, "We retained the original footprint of the old structures fully believing that 300 years ago buildings respected the topography, the seasons, and the movement of the sun."

This is Cornelia's second career; she had worked in finance in the Middle East. Originally from England, she met and married an Italian. When she reinvented herself, Italy was the only choice for them. They have five boys who all work on the property in some capacity. Her husband, Corrado, works abroad, but when he's on the farm he is happiest on his tractor!

Cornelia is training their eldest son, Luca, age twenty, to run the restaurant. He's just graduated from hospitality school. Cornelia says, "Our mission at the restaurant is to make everything in-house, from local and seasonal ingredients. We use traditional recipes and add our own twist to lighten what have been historically heavy dishes intended to feed a poor starving farming and hunting population. We aim for zero waste by offering small daily menus; any leftovers are used to feed the family, staff, [and] animals and we compost the rest."

Cornelia works to include ancient recipes from their region in Pontremoli, in the heart of Lunigiana. They use truffles in many of their dishes, including rabbit, egg yolk ravioli, as a dressing to beef tagliata, or even in desserts, such as white truffle panna cotta with white chocolate. Most of their plates are finished off with a drizzle of their own organic EVOO.

She graciously agreed to lend a recipe to this book—this is a favorite, with truffles and rabbit and chestnuts. It is, of course, local and authentic, but with a little twist via the added pecorino cream and radicchio.

WOOD-GRILLED LAMB CHOPS
with Porcini Mushrooms
(BISTECCHINE DI AGNELLO ALLA BRACE)

Fresh lamb is available year-round in Lunigiana. If you like the grilled steak with arugula that I serve in the summertime (recipe, page 82), you'll love this dish — it's a heartier, autumnal version. Marinating the lamb in garlic, vinegar, and oil gives it a rich, caramel-like flavor. When I grill large mushrooms, I leave the stems on because they're as delicious as the caps. Most people think old mushrooms should be thrown out, but, actually, grilling is a great use for slightly older mushrooms, since the high heat concentrates their stronger flavor.

Serves 6 to 8

2 cloves garlic, minced

¼ cup balsamic vinegar

1 cup extra virgin olive oil

3 tablespoons chopped fresh rosemary

1 teaspoon salt

½ teaspoon freshly ground black pepper

12 to 16 lamb chops (about 4 pounds)

12 to 16 whole porcini, or 20 cremini or baby bella mushrooms

8 cups loosely packed fresh arugula

1 cup shaved Parmesan cheese

In a large bowl, combine the garlic, vinegar, olive oil, rosemary, salt, and pepper, then divide the marinade equally between 2 zip-tight bags. Place half the lamb chops and mushrooms in each bag, seal, and refrigerate for at least 4 hours or as long as overnight. Bring to room temperature before grilling.

Prepare a grill for direct cooking, or preheat a gas grill to medium-high heat, 350 to 400°F. If using a charcoal grill, the grill is ready when the charcoal turns white, about 1 hour after lighting the coals. Clean your grate and let it heat at least 10 minutes before cooking.

Place the mushrooms and the lamb chops onto the grill rack. Grill for 3 to 5 minutes on each side, until the mushrooms are soft and the lamb chops are seared.

On a platter, make a bed of the arugula. Add the chops and mushrooms, and top the arugula with shaved Parmesan. Serve warm.

LA FORTEZZA BOLOGNESE SAUCE

I know, I know, Bologna isn't in Lunigiana, but this dish is popular worldwide. At La Fortezza I always have a pot of this sauce going on the stove. Our guests expect it to be served when they visit. Not only is it great on all variations of pasta, but I use any leftovers on our wood-fired pizza too. This is our most popular pizza topping.
Grass-fed beef is much better than choice or prime when it comes to flavor. Make sure you form it into a 1-inch-thick patty and brown it on both sides before you break it up with a heatproof spatula. Don't break it up before you brown it—the meat will stay moist as it cooks. ✂ ***Makes 6 cups***

½ cup extra virgin olive oil

1 pound ground beef (at least 15% fat)

4 stalks celery, chopped

1 medium carrot, peeled and chopped

1 small yellow onion, chopped

1 teaspoon salt

2 cloves garlic, minced

1 (14-ounce) can Mutti Polpa chopped tomatoes, or another good-quality brand

Place the olive oil in a 4-quart Dutch oven over medium heat. Add the ground beef in one piece to one side of the pot. Add the celery, carrot, onion, and salt on the other side of the pot while the beef browns. Sauté the meat for 8 to 10 minutes until deep brown, then flip, making sure to keep the piece whole, and brown it on the other side, about 5 minutes. Meanwhile, stir the vegetables and sauté until they are a nice brown color.

Stir the garlic into the vegetables and break up the ground beef with a spatula, mixing it in with the vegetables as well. Once the mixture is thoroughly combined, add the tomatoes with their juice. Let the sauce cook down gently, stirring occasionally, for about 45 minutes or until it has reduced by half. I like to serve this with homemade pappardelle pasta made using the Basic Egg Pasta Dough (recipe, page 30).

LA FORTEZZA PIZZA

I make pizza in our forno every Sunday, for ourselves or for our frequent guests. Over the years, I've perfected the recipe for this dough. Pizza research—I dig it! The most important piece of equipment to own is a peel, the paddle you use to get the pizza into and out of the oven. The dough needs to sit at room temperature for 1 to 6 hours before making pizza. You can make the dough in the morning, cover with plastic wrap, and allow it to rise all day, or let it rise in the refrigerator overnight. This is a good tip to make the dough the day before as the refrigerator slows the rise and makes it perfect the next day. From the refrigerator let it come to room temperature, which will take at least 1 hour. At home in Atlanta, I don't have a pizza oven, so I put the pizza stone on our gas grill, close the lid, and heat it to close to 700°F, which cooks the pizza in 6 minutes and gives the crust a good char. Pizza stones are great to use in the oven as well. I just have found I can get my grill much hotter, closer to the temperature of my pizza oven in Italy. Make sure you heat the stone for at least 20 minutes in the oven or on the grill before making your pizza. You can find pizza stones at any cooking retail store or online. Compressed or brick yeast is fresh yeast that is perfect for making breads that take a long time to rise because I find it activates more quickly than dry yeast. It is sold in very small compressed blocks, about 1 by 1 ½ inches. It is made from cream yeast, from which a good deal of the water has been removed by centrifugal force. It is moist (about 70 percent moisture), crumbly, and creamy white. You can find the little foil-wrapped cakes in the refrigerated sections of many grocery stores. I don't recommend freezing half the pizza dough—use it immediately.

Makes two (12-inch) pizzas

....

1 ½ tablespoons crumbled brick yeast, or 1 envelope (2 ¼ teaspoons) active dry yeast

6 cups 00 flour, plus more for the work surface

1 cup extra virgin olive oil, plus more for the bowl

1 ½ teaspoons salt

Pizza toppings, as desired

1 cup semolina flour or cornmeal, for dusting the peel (paddle)

....

In the bowl of a standing mixer fitted with the dough hook, mix 1 cup warm water with the yeast. Once mixed, let it sit for about 10 minutes to bloom—because it's fresh yeast you won't see bubbles; with dry yeast you will see bubbles. Add the flour, oil, and salt and knead with the dough hook for 5 minutes, adding a little more warm water by the spoonful if the dough seems dry; it should be soft to the touch, but not sticky.

Transfer the dough to a lightly floured work surface and knead for about 2 minutes by hand, then form a large ball. Place the dough ball into a large oiled bowl and cover tightly with plastic wrap. Let it sit for at least 1 hour at room temperature to rise or up to 6 hours until tripled in size. The dough can also be refrigerated overnight.

Preheat a conventional oven to 500°F with the pizza stone on the middle rack.

Divide the dough in half and roll out each half into a 12-inch-diameter round about ½ inch thick.

Top the dough rounds with your desired pizza ingredients. Using a peel sprinkled with semolina flour, transfer the dough into the oven, directly onto the pizza stone. Cook for 10 to 15 minutes, rotating halfway through baking to cook evenly. Use the peel again to pull the pizza out, and let it cool for 5 minutes before slicing.

If using a gas grill, heat it to 700°F. Place the pizza stone directly on the grill, preheat for about 20 minutes, and then bake the pizza for about 6 minutes.

APPLE FRITTERS
(FRITTELLE DOLCI CON LE MELE)

I really enjoy using honey and apples in a dessert, and these would be great for the Jewish High Holidays, because apples dipped in honey mean "Have a sweet new year." There's a big synagogue in La Spezia and I go there with my friend Jacob. I've found that in most port towns in Italy, there's a beautiful synagogue. Granny Smith apples are great for this recipe because they are both crisp and tart. ✂ **Serves 6**

2 cups milk

2 large eggs

2 tablespoons sugar

1 teaspoon salt, divided

¾ cup all-purpose flour

1 teaspoon baking powder

2 apples (I use Granny Smith)

Juice of 1 lemon

3 to 4 cups sunflower oil, for frying

Confectioners' sugar or honey, for serving

In the bowl of a standing mixer fitted with the paddle attachment, beat the milk, eggs, sugar, and salt together until well combined, about 3 minutes.

In a separate bowl, sift the flour and the baking powder. On low speed, add the flour mixture into the egg mixture until just combined. Set aside to let the batter rest at room temperature for 30 minutes.

Peel and core the apples. Slice crosswise into rings about ¾ inch thick. Toss the apple slices in a shallow bowl with the lemon juice to coat.

In a large Dutch oven, bring the oil to 325°F over high heat. Toss in a little batter: If it sizzles, you're ready to fry.

Dip the apples into the batter to coat them completely. Using a spider strainer or slotted spoon, slide the apple rings slowly into the hot oil, three at a time (do not crowd the pot), and fry for 5 minutes. Flip the fritters and fry for 3 minutes on the other side. Once brown on all sides and lightly puffed, remove to paper towels to drain.

Transfer to a platter, sprinkle with confectioners' sugar or honey, and serve immediately.

WALNUT RAISIN SWEET BREAD
(BUCCELLATO)

This dense, sweet bread is always a winner with a crowd. It's a local recipe that originally hails from nearby Lucca, though it's similar to Milanese panettone. The freeform dough doesn't require a pan to bake, and the egg wash makes it golden brown and shiny. ✄ ***Makes one 13-inch round cake***

2 tablespoons crumbled brick yeast

1 cup sugar

1 egg yolk

5 tablespoons unsalted butter, at room temperature

3 ½ cups all-purpose flour

½ cup walnuts, toasted

¼ cup plus 1 tablespoon raisins

1 teaspoon salt

3 tablespoons extra virgin olive oil

1 egg yolk beaten with 2 tablespoons water, for egg wash

In the bowl of a standing mixer fitted with the dough hook, combine the yeast with 1 cup warm water and blend on low speed for 30 seconds to mix. Let the mixture rest at room temperature for 10 minutes to activate.

Add the sugar, egg yolk, and butter and mix until smooth. Then add the flour on low speed and continue to mix for about 5 minutes, until the dough is smooth and elastic. Add the walnuts, raisins, and salt and mix just until combined.

Coat a bowl with the olive oil, and coat your hands with olive oil as well. Use your hands to shape the dough into a ball. Place in the bowl, cover with plastic wrap, and let the dough rise at room temperature until it has doubled in size, about 3 hours.

Transfer the risen dough to a lightly floured work surface. Use your hands to pat it out, then roll the dough out to form a 3 by 14-inch log.

Set a short water glass, 3 inches in diameter, upside-down in the center of a parchment-lined baking sheet. Wrap the dough log around the glass to form a ring. Remove the glass, and let the dough rise uncovered at room temperature for 1 hour—it won't quite double in size again.

Preheat the oven to 350°F. Brush the top of the ring with the egg wash and bake for about 1 hour until golden brown, and a toothpick inserted in the center comes out clean.

Let it cool slightly, then serve warm or at room temperature with butter and Giovanna's Grape Jam (recipe follows).

NOTE ABOUT PRESERVING

How do you know when your jars are properly sealed when canning or preserving? There are two types of jars you can use for the canning recipes n this book.

1. A glass jar with a metal lid that twists off

These lids are sealed when the middle of the lid has an indentation. If any of your jars do not have a proper indentation, you can refrigerate those and consume them first. They will keep in the refrigerator for a few months. The rest of the sealed jars will keep in your pantry for 1 year.

2. A Weck jar with a glass top, a rubber sealing gasket, and metal clips

Once the jars are pulled from the water, allow them to cool completely. Once cooled, if you can hold the glass lid of the jar without it opening, the jar is sealed. When you want to break the seal, simply pull on the rubber seal; there is a tab. It will release the seal.

GIOVANNA'S GRAPE JAM
(MARMELLATA DI UVA)

My son claims this is the best grape jam he has ever tasted. In fact, he ate an entire jar with a spoon—"No bread neces-sary," he said. I will say, it's pretty spectacular, and I am thinking the secret ingredients are the lemon and apple that brighten the flavor and give it a thick richness and consistency. The skins of the grapes and apples contribute natural pectin, so there's no need to add more. Grazie mille, Giovanna, for sharing this magical recipe. Although it's slightly unconventional, I do not remove the seeds, finding that I enjoy the added crunch.

Makes four 6-ounce jars

2 pounds purple grapes

4 cups sugar

Juice of 1 lemon

1 apple, cored and chopped

Wash the grapes, cut them in half, and remove the seeds if you'd like (see note above). In a heavy saucepan, combine the grapes with the sugar, lemon juice, and apple. Set over low heat, bring to a simmer, and cook for 1 hour, until the mixture is quite thick. Let cool then process once through a food mill set over a large bowl to separate out the skins.

Fill a large pot one-third full of water and heat on the stovetop until a thermometer reads 180°F.

Check the jars, lids, and bands for proper function-ing, and place them in the hot water for 10 minutes to sterilize. Use a jar lifter to remove the preheated jars and place on a clean cloth towel to drain. Fill the jars with jam to ½ inch from the top, and tighten and test the lids.

These jars will keep in the pantry for up to 1 year. Refrigerate after opening.

PEAR TART
with Multigrain Crust

We are surrounded by pear trees at La Fortezza, and when they ripen in the autumn, the fruit is the most delicious I have ever tasted. I make jam and this tart is always a hit. The amazing 7-grain flour, which has the rich qualities of rye flour, comes from the Moro, a local mill. I enjoy this delicious tart with a cappuccino for breakfast.

Serves 8

For the crust:

1 stick (8 tablespoons) chilled salted butter, divided

3 cups 7-grain flour (see Source Guide, page 205) or rye flour, plus more for the work surface

1 tablespoon turbinado sugar

For the pear puree:

6 pears, divided

2 tablespoons granulated sugar

½ teaspoon salt

Juice of 1 lemon

2 tablespoons turbinado sugar

To prepare the crust: Combine 7 tablespoons butter, 3 cups flour, and sugar in a food processor fitted with a metal blade and blend until the mixture has the consistency of grainy sand. Add ½ cup ice water and blend until the mixture forms a soft, pliable dough, adding additional water as needed if the dough seems dry. Turn the dough out onto a lightly floured work surface and form into a disk. Wrap the dough in plastic wrap and chill for at least 30 minutes. The dough can also be stored in the refrigerator for up to 2 days.

Preheat the oven to 350°F. Grease a 12-inch tart pan with the remaining 1 tablespoon butter.

Prepare a lightly floured work surface and roll the chilled dough out to a 15-inch round, about ¼ inch thick. Using your fingers, carefully press the dough into the prepared pan—don't be concerned if the dough breaks; it's slightly brittle, but easy to press back together. Clean the edges of the pan with a knife, then cover with plastic wrap and freeze for at least 30 minutes before baking. The crust can also be stored in the freezer for up to 2 months.

To prepare the puree: Peel, core, and chop 2 pears into 1-inch pieces. In a small pot over medium heat, combine the chopped pears with the granulated sugar, salt, and ¼ cup water and cook for 10 minutes until the fruit is soft. Set aside to cool.

Transfer the cooled pears with their cooking liquid into a food processor fitted with a metal blade and blend until smooth. (This can be done while the crust is in the freezer). Set aside to cool for about 30 minutes, then spread the pear puree into the frozen crust.

Peel, core, and thinly slice the remaining 4 pears. Toss the sliced pears in a bowl with the lemon juice, then, starting on the outer edge of the tart, arrange the slices in a pinwheel shape on top of the pear puree. Sprinkle with the turbinado sugar. Before baking, place the composed tart back into the freezer for 15 minutes.

Transfer to the oven and bake for 50 minutes to 1 hour, until golden brown.

Let cool slightly and serve warm or at room temperature. This tart keeps, covered, at room temperature for up to 2 days.

Inverno

WINTER
RECISES

CHICKPEA SOUP
with Pancetta and Sage
(ZUPPA DI CECI)

Chickpeas are used a lot in the food of the region and are a great source of vegetable protein. I always think of this as the Italian version of "stone soup," an example of cucina povera *("food of the poor"), a term used when simple, less expensive ingredients are used in a dish. These humble ingredients can create a very satisfying and delicious meal. For vegetarians, you can omit the pancetta and still have a nutritious soup.*

Serves 6 to 8

2 cups dried chickpeas, or 3 cups canned chickpeas

3 tablespoons extra virgin olive oil

8 ounces pancetta, diced (1 cup)

2 carrots, peeled and diced

2 stalks celery, diced

1 small onion, diced

2 tablespoons thinly sliced fresh sage

1 teaspoon salt

½ teaspoon freshly ground pepper

8 cups vegetable broth

Soak the dried chickpeas in cold water for 12 hours, then rinse them under tap water. If you are using canned, drain and rinse the chickpeas.

In a stockpot over medium heat, add the oil, pancetta, carrots, celery, onion, sage, salt, and pepper. Sauté for about 10 minutes until the vegetables are soft. Add the chickpeas and the broth, reduce the heat to low, and simmer for 3 hours (2 hours if using canned chickpeas).

Remove 1 cup of the soup, place in a blender, and blend to a creamy consistency. Return it to the soup for a more satiny texture. Serve warm with Cà Vidè Focaccia (recipe, page 187), or your choice of bread.

POTATOES ROASTED IN OLIVE OIL, GARLIC, AND HERBS

I was amazed at the quality of potatoes in Lunigiana. I first bought them at a local winter market. It was bitter cold outside and I was in need of some comfort food, so I decided to roast a chicken with vegetables and potatoes. The potatoes had the texture of butter and were easy to slice, yet still crisp and very fresh. Who knew a simple potato could give so much joy? This is a versatile potato side dish, and you can either cook the potatoes peel-on or peeled, it's your choice. They will be delicious either way. I like to blanch the potatoes before roasting them; this technique makes them even crispier.

Serves 6 to 8

3 pounds small red or white potatoes, cut into 2-inch pieces

¼ cup extra virgin olive oil

1 ½ teaspoons kosher salt

1 teaspoon freshly ground black pepper

2 tablespoons chopped fresh rosemary

1 tablespoon dried oregano

6 whole cloves garlic

Preheat the oven to 400°F.

Fill a large pot with enough water to cover the potatoes and bring to a boil over high heat, then reduce the heat to medium and simmer the potatoes for 15 minutes until they are tender but firm. Drain the potatoes and pat dry with a kitchen towel.

Place the potatoes in a bowl with the olive oil, salt, pepper, rosemary, oregano, and garlic and toss until well coated. Transfer the potatoes to a sheet pan and spread out into one layer.

Roast for 45 minutes to 1 hour, or until browned and crisp. Turn with a spatula during cooking in order to ensure even browning. Serve hot.

WARM KALE SALAD
with Tomato and Chickpeas

This recipe came from picking the remnants of the garden. Our tomato plants hang out sometimes until November with a few tomatoes on them. I laughingly called it our leftover garden salad, but now I serve it all the time at La Fortezza because it's such a hit with guests. It's simple and easy, and it's vegetarian approved. **Serves 4 to 6**

¼ cup extra virgin olive oil

1 small red onion, thinly sliced

10 cups loosely packed shredded kale

2 cups cherry tomatoes

1 cup canned chickpeas, rinsed and drained

1 teaspoon salt

¼ cup red wine vinegar

Juice of ½ lemon

In a large shallow pan on low heat, warm the oil and add the onion, kale, tomatoes, and chickpeas. Toss together for about 3 minutes, until the kale is wilted. Add the salt, vinegar, and lemon juice and serve warm.

ROASTED CARROTS
with Grated Bottarga and Dressed in Lemon Juice and Olive Oil

Bottarga is a delicacy of dried, salted, cured fish roe, typically from the grey mullet or bluefin tuna. It is considered to be the truffle of the sea, and is used as a condiment in lieu of salt—sprinkled on pasta, pizza, and vegetables (as in this recipe). In fact, it's way more potent than salt; it's a big umami blast. It is one of those very Italian ingredients that you may think is hard to find outside of Italy, but it's not (see Source Guide, page 205). A staple in my La Fortezza pantry, it's sold in a small brick that can be grated or comes already grated in a jar.

Serves 4

12 small carrots (about 1 pound)
6 tablespoons extra virgin olive oil, divided
Juice of 1 lemon
3 tablespoons grated bottarga

Preheat the oven to 400°F.

Clean and peel the carrots, place them into a roasting pan, and drizzle with 3 tablespoons olive oil. Shake the pan to coat them completely. Bake for 30 minutes, or until the carrots are fork tender.

Transfer them to a platter, drizzle with the lemon juice and the remaining 3 tablespoons olive oil, and sprinkle them with the bottarga. Serve warm.

CHESTNUT GNOCCHI
with Pecorino and Chard

This is the perfect comfort food. Plus it is a great repurpose recipe. Since Italians firmly believe in no waste, recipes like this one use leftover mashed potatoes. Most people think it's hard to make gnocchi, but it's not. Admittedly, it's a commitment of a couple of hours, but you can double the recipe and freeze half for another meal. I like using the chestnut flour for the pasta, which gives the gnocchi a nutty taste and a satisfying chewy texture. Instead of just boiling the gnocchi, they are sautéed in butter and olive oil, so they're a little crispy outside and velvety soft inside.

Serves 4

For the gnocchi:

3 pounds russet potatoes (about 6 medium)

1 tablespoon salt, plus ¼ cup for cooking the pasta

2 large eggs

1 cup chestnut flour, sifted

2 cups all-purpose flour, divided

For the chard:

¼ cup extra virgin olive oil

2 tablespoons unsalted butter

6 cups thinly sliced chard

1 cup shaved pecorino or Parmesan cheese

To prepare the gnocchi: Boil the potatoes for 15 minutes, until just tender, and drain. Let cool enough to handle, then peel. Pass the potatoes one at a time through a ricer into a large bowl, then spread the riced potatoes onto a baking sheet, sprinkle with 1 tablespoon salt, and let the potatoes cool and dry for 30 minutes. Once cool, transfer to a large mixing bowl. Note: If you're using leftover mashed potatoes you can just jump to this next step.

Whisk the eggs in a small bowl and drizzle them over the potatoes. Using a fork, gently stir to combine. Sift the chestnut flour over the mixture, stirring with the fork to incorporate. Stir in the all-purpose flour until just combined. Knead the dough for about 5 minutes, until it is soft but holds together; it should not crack, but have the consistency of room temperature butter.

Divide the dough into two 5-inch disks, then divide each disk into quarters. Roll each quarter into a 12-inch rope, about 1 inch in diameter. Cut the rope into 1-inch lengths and, using the tines of a fork or a ribbed gnocchi board, gently roll the gnocchi to form ridges.

Fill a large pot three-fourths full of water, add the salt, and bring to a boil over high heat. Cook the gnocchi in 4 batches so they won't crowd the pot and stick to each other.

While the gnocchi are cooking, heat a large skillet on medium-low and add the oil and butter.

Use a spider strainer or slotted spoon to remove the gnocchi after about 3 minutes, when they float to the top, and add them directly to the warm skillet.

Once all the batches are in the skillet, increase the heat to medium-high and cook for about 3 minutes, turning to brown overall. Then toss in the chard and cook for about 3 minutes, until it is wilted but still with a bite.

Divide into individual bowls and top with the pecorino. Serve immediately.

BAVETTE PASTA
with Anchovy
(BAVETTE CON L'ACCIUGATA/
BAVETE KON L'AZUGATA)

Bavette is a flat, narrow ribbon noodle similar to linguine but with a convex shape. This type of pasta originates in Genoa, and is the most typical cut of Ligurian pasta. Bavette pasta is frequently paired with a pesto sauce, which is also a Ligurian creation, and it is traditionally served with this dish.
I love the combination of butter and anchovies in this recipe—it's like eating anchovies on buttered bread, which most Italians remember as a traditional snack from childhood. This surprisingly elegant pantry pasta has all the comfort of eating at your nonna's table. **Serves 4**

¾ cup salted anchovy fillets

4 tablespoons salted butter

¼ cup plus 2 tablespoons extra virgin olive oil

1 clove garlic, minced

1 fresh Calabrian hot pepper, finely chopped, or 1 teaspoon red pepper flakes

¼ cup salt, for cooking the pasta

18 ounces dried bavette pasta (Source Guide, page 205)

1 cup chopped fresh flat-leaf parsley, for garnish

Rinse the anchovies and pat dry with a paper towel. In a large saucepan, melt the butter with the olive oil over low heat. Chop the anchovies and add them to the pot. Cook over low heat for about 2 minutes, just to warm them, then add the garlic and mash the anchovies into the garlic; add the hot pepper and stir to combine. Remove from heat, cover, and keep warm while you make the pasta.

Fill a large pot three-quarters full of water, add the salt, and bring to a boil over medium-high heat. Add the pasta and cook until al dente.

Transfer the anchovy sauce to a warmed serving bowl. When the pasta is ready, use a slotted spoon or spider strainer to transfer it to the bowl and toss to combine. Garnish with the parsley. Serve warm.

TAGLIATELLE
with Leeks
(TAGLIATELLE AI PORRI)

Leeks are grown everywhere in the region; they are of the onion family and love the cooler climate of the mountains. An underused vegetable in the United States, leeks are more prevalent in markets around Lunigiana. I didn't use them very much until we moved here. They have a more subtle taste than an onion, so I use them in soups, or with potatoes, and with pasta, to add a delicate onion flavor. This is a classic pasta dish in the region, and really features the flavor of these popular vegetables.

To clean and prepare the leeks, remove the root end and the top green part of the leeks and discard, then thinly slice the length crosswise. The layers of a leek often hold a good amount of dirt, so transfer the slices to a large bowl of cool water to cover and soak for 30 minutes. The leek pieces will float to the top, so just scoop them off with your hand or a slotted spoon, leaving the dirt at the bottom. Drain and repeat the process.

Serves 4

¼ cup extra virgin olive oil

5 tablespoons unsalted butter

1 ½ cups tomato sauce (recipe, page 76)

½ cup chopped fresh flat-leaf parsley

1 teaspoon chopped fresh rosemary

1 teaspoon salt, plus ¼ cup for cooking the pasta

½ teaspoon freshly ground black pepper

3 ½ cups thinly sliced leeks (about 2 large)

¼ cup sliced button mushrooms

Basic Egg Pasta Dough (recipe, page 30)

⅓ cup grated Parmesan cheese

In a large skillet over medium heat, stir in the oil, butter, tomato sauce, parsley, rosemary, salt, and pepper and cook for 3 minutes. Add the leeks and mushrooms, reduce the heat to low, and simmer for 1 hour.

Make the pasta dough, roll out, and cut into ¼-inch-wide tagliatelle.

Fill a large pot with water, add the salt, and bring to a rolling boil over high heat, then add the pasta and cook for 3 to 5 minutes until al dente. Drain with a spider strainer or slotted spoon, add to the leek mixture, and toss quickly over heat. Serve in bowls and top with Parmesan cheese.

ORECCHIETTE
with Broccoli Rabe and Sausage
(ORECCHIETTE CON RAPINI E SALSICCIA)

Orecchiette means "little ears," and that's what this pasta resembles. It's bite-size, and a bit thicker than most pastas, which makes it chewy. It takes a little longer to cook, but is very easy to work with. The cup shape holds any chunky sauce well. If you aren't a fan of bitter vegetables, substitute broccoli for the broccoli rabe. In Lunigiana the sausage is outstanding. This area is known for excellent sausages made with fennel seeds, cloves, and black pepper. You can add a small amount of these spices to re-create the flavor of these sausages as they cook and get a more authentic flavor. 🌿 *Serves 4*

8 ounces broccoli rabe, cut into bite-size pieces (2 to 3 cups)

¼ cup plus 1 teaspoon salt, divided

1 pound dried orecchiette

⅓ cup extra virgin olive oil

2 pounds Italian sausage, sweet, hot, or a combination, casings removed

3 large cloves garlic, minced

1 teaspoon red pepper flakes

1 teaspoon dried fennel seeds

1 teaspoon freshly ground black pepper

½ teaspoon finely ground cloves

1 cup grated Parmesan cheese, for serving

Fill a large pot three-quarters full with water and bring to a rolling boil over high heat. Add the broccoli rabe and cook for 2 to 3 minutes, testing often, just until the stems are tender. Use tongs or a wire-mesh skimmer to transfer the broccoli rabe to a colander, and run it under cold water to stop the cooking process. Set aside.

Keep the pot of water at a full boil and add ¼ cup salt. Add the pasta and cook until al dente.

In a large skillet over medium-low heat, warm the olive oil. Add the sausage, garlic, red pepper flakes, fennel seeds, black pepper, and cloves and cook for about 7 minutes, stirring and breaking up the sausage meat with a wooden spoon, until the sausage is thoroughly browned. Add the broccoli rabe and stir to combine. Cook for 2 minutes, until hot throughout.

When the pasta is ready, use a slotted spoon or a spider skimmer to transfer it to the skillet with the sausage and broccoli rabe. With the heat reduced to low, stir in the remaining 1 teaspoon salt. Add some of the pasta cooking water if the mixture seems dry. Serve warm with grated Parmesan.

MUSSELS IN TOMATO SAUCE
with Bacon-Breadcrumb Stuffing
(COZZE RIPIENE)

I've never tasted these stuffed mussels anywhere other than Italy. A friend ordered them at a restaurant in Carrara, and I had to ask the chef, "How in the world do you stuff a mussel?" I learned that you must crack them open, remove and chop the mussel, mix the mussels with the herby breadcrumbs, return it to the bottom half shell, and replace the top shell. Then they're tied up and baked in the oven—similar to oysters Rockefeller. It is a beloved dish in the region, served at all the fishmongers' restaurants along the coast. ✂ *Serves 6 to 8*

40 large mussels
¼ cup chopped fresh flat-leaf parsley
1 clove garlic, minced
⅓ cup breadcrumbs made from day-old bread
1 cup milk
2 large eggs
½ cup chopped soft salami, such as Genoa salami

1 teaspoon salt
½ teaspoon freshly ground black pepper
¾ cup grated Parmesan cheese
¼ cup plus 1 tablespoon extra virgin olive oil
1 ½ cups chopped tomatoes (2 large tomatoes)
½ cup red wine

Preheat the oven to 375°F.

Clean and wash the mussels and debeard them (the beard is a fiber that you pull off). Using a paring or shucking knife, open the shell. Holding the mussel securely with a kitchen towel to prevent slipping, carefully remove the mussel flesh with the knife; reserving the shells.

Chop the removed mussels and mix them with the parsley and garlic in a small bowl. Rinse the shells, dry with a towel, and set aside.

In a separate bowl, soak the breadcrumbs in the milk for 10 minutes. Squeeze out all the excess milk with your hands, and add the bread to the mussel mixture. Add the eggs, salami, salt, pepper, and cheese and mix well.

Arrange the bottom shells on a baking sheet. Place 1 tablespoon of the stuffing mixture into each shell, cover with the top shell, and tie securely with kitchen twine. Transfer the stuffed mussels to a 4-quart casserole with a lid and top with the olive oil, tomatoes, and red wine. Cover and bake for 40 minutes. Serve warm.

Note: There's no need to remove the twine before serving; it is easier to remove right before eating.

Mussel Farmer of La Spezia, Paolo Varrella

I had never heard of a mussel farmer before I came to Italy, and I love mussels, so I made a point of meeting Paolo so he could show me what his work involves. He's been a mussel farmer for two decades and is known as the "DJ mussel farmer" because of the tunes he spins as he motors out into the Bay of Poets to haul his catch.

It's tough work, as I discovered. The first thing I saw was a gridwork of buoys bobbing in the bay. Long ropes attached to these buoys provide the fabric for mussels to attach themselves. Paolo works alongside a friend who dives to retrieves the heavy, mussel-laden ropes, and hauls them into his boat. Once collected, the mussels are taken to a floating platform fitted with a cleaning machine for a first cleaning. The sound is deafening as the high-power rinse removes the first layer of grit from the shells. Then the mussels are taken to an industrial cleaning facility that bags the mussels into forty-pound sacks. It's a bustling place every day, with boats lining up to unload and clean their hauls. Riding with Paolo for the first time was an experience I will never forget. Working with fresh mussels plucked from the sea only hours before they are cooked is something that makes living so near the seaside just incredible.

OVEN-ROASTED TROUT
with White Wine and Herbs
(TROTA AL FORNO)

Trout fishing is popular in the streams, lakes, and mountain rivers of Lunigiana. There's a fishmonger who brings a refrigerated truck to our weekly market. He usually offers local trout, as well as the catch from La Spezia—branzino, cod, sea bass, mussels, and calamari. This recipe calls for oven roasting but achieves the same crispy skin and delicate meat as from grilling. Ask your fishmonger to clean the trout for you. ✺ *Serves 4*

4 (1-pound) whole trout, cleaned

1 teaspoon chopped fresh rosemary

1 teaspoon chopped fresh thyme

½ cup chopped fresh flat-leaf parsley

1 teaspoon chopped fresh oregano

1 small shallot, finely diced

2 tablespoons unsalted butter, at room temperature

½ teaspoon salt

½ teaspoon freshly ground black pepper

2 tablespoons extra virgin olive oil

½ cup white wine

1 lemon, sliced, for serving

Preheat the oven to 350°F.

Wash and pat the fish dry, inside and out.

In a small bowl, combine the rosemary, thyme, parsley, and oregano with the shallot, butter, salt, and pepper until well combined. Divide the herbed butter into 4 portions and fill the cavity of each fish with it, then transfer them to a baking sheet lined with parchment paper. Drizzle them with the olive oil and wine.

Bake for 20 to 25 minutes, until the fish is firm to the touch and the skin is crispy.

Transfer to a platter and serve warm with lemon slices.

BOAR STEW
with Polenta

Wild boar, or cinghiale *in Italian, yields a dark red meat that looks more like beef than pork. It's very lean, and reminds me of bison, which, of course, means that it can be tough and gamey if not properly prepared. The local boars' appetite for grasses, chestnuts, figs, mushrooms, and truffles—they have a very sophisticated diet— gives their meat a unique flavor, almost like a terroir as expressed in wine. I treat boar meat like a brisket and cook it slowly; the result is a moist stew layered with rich, woodsy flavors. Order boar meat from your butcher or check the Source Guide (see page 205). You can serve same day, or I like to let it cool and then refrigerate for a day to let the flavors develop and deepen—plus, the meat will become more tender. Heat thoroughly before serving.*
✖ *Serves 8 to 10*

For the marinade:

1 (8-ounce) jar sundried tomatoes in oil

8 cloves garlic

¼ cup dried oregano

¼ cup chopped fresh rosemary

¼ cup balsamic vinegar

2 teaspoons salt

1 teaspoon white pepper

½ teaspoon freshly ground black pepper

4 pounds wild boar, cut into 1 ½-inch cubes

For the stew:

3 tablespoons extra virgin olive oil

2 carrots, cut into coins

2 stalks celery, cut into 1-inch pieces

1 medium onion, chopped

2 cups red wine

2 cups beef broth

1 (28-ounce) can Mutti Polpa crushed tomatoes, or another good-quality brand

For serving:

Polenta for serving 8 to 10 (recipe, page 42)

Fresh flat-leaf parsley, for garnish

To marinate the boar: In the bowl of a food processor fitted with a metal blade, combine the sundried tomatoes and their oil, the garlic, oregano, rosemary, balsamic vinegar, salt, white pepper, and black pepper. Blend the marinade until well mixed.

Place the meat and marinade in a large bowl and mix thoroughly to make sure the boar is evenly coated, then transfer into a 1-gallon zip-tight bag (you may need two bags). Seal and refrigerate for at least 8 hours, or overnight.

To make the stew: Preheat the oven to 300°F.

Remove the boar from the marinade and place it on a plate, reserving the marinade.

Pour the oil into a large Dutch oven over high heat. When the pot heats up, reduce the heat to medium and add the meat in batches, in one layer, making sure not to overcrowd the pan. Cook each batch for 10 minutes, turning the meat with tongs until browned on all sides. Remove the browned meat to a plate.

Add the carrots, celery, and onion to the Dutch oven. Stirring and scraping up the browned bits from the meat with a wooden spoon, cook for 10 minutes until the vegetables have softened. Add the wine and broth and deglaze the pan.

Return the meat to the Dutch oven with the vegetables, and add the reserved marinade and the crushed tomatoes. Bring to a simmer, stir, and cover. Transfer to the oven and bake for 4 to 6 hours. (Most Italians leave it in the oven all day,

or up to 8 hours.) The longer it cooks, the more tender the meat is. The meat should be fork tender and surrounded by a rich sauce. Be sure to check often and add water as needed so the boar meat doesn't dry out.

As the stew cooks, make the polenta.

To serve, spoon 1 ½ cups cooked polenta into each shallow bowl, top with 2 cups of the boar stew, and garnish with fresh parsley.

RABBIT
with Apples and Chestnut Gnocchi
(CONIGLIO ALLE MELE CON GNOCCHI DI CASTAGNE)

We have a lot of apple trees in our orchard and use apples frequently in savory dishes as well as sweet ones. I prefer sour apples for this recipe—the tang adds a great spark of flavor to cut through the buttery chestnut gnocchi. We harvest fennel pollen in the fall—a golden powdery substance that can be used to subtly season dishes such as this. In the winter, the fennel goes to seed, and that's when we harvest the seeds. The fennel seed perfectly complements the taste of the rabbit and sour apples. Ask your butcher to break down the rabbits for you; or you may substitute chicken pieces.

Serves 4

---

6 tart apples, such as Pink Lady or Granny Smith

3 tablespoons extra virgin olive oil

8 ounces pancetta, chopped (1 cup)

1 large onion, chopped

1 tablespoon crushed fennel seeds

3 sprigs fresh rosemary

2 (1½-pound) rabbits, each broken down into 6 to 8 bone-in pieces, or 1 (3-pound) chicken, cut into 6 to 8 bone-in pieces

2 cups white wine, plus more as needed

1 teaspoon salt

½ teaspoon freshly ground black pepper

Chestnut Gnocchi (recipe, page 164)

2 tablespoons unsalted butter

2 tablespoons fresh lemon juice (about ½ lemon)

1 cup chopped fresh flat-leaf parsley

1 teaspoon fennel pollen

Preheat the oven to 350°F.

Peel, core, and cut the apples into 2-inch pieces.

In a large Dutch oven over medium heat, warm the oil and sauté the pancetta and onion for 7 to 10 minutes, until the onion is soft and lightly caramelized. Reduce the heat to low and add the apples, fennel seeds, rosemary, the rabbit pieces, wine, salt, and pepper and stir. Cover and roast for 2 to 3 hours, until the rabbit is tender. Halfway through cooking, check the liquid and add more wine as needed.

Prepare the chestnut gnocchi and cook them in boiling water according to instructions.

To serve, toss the cooked and drained gnocchi with butter on a warmed platter and place the rabbit pieces with their juices over the gnocchi. Sprinkle with lemon juice, chopped parsley, and fennel pollen and serve warm.

Shepherdess of Zeri, Cinzia Rossano

The Zeri lamb exists only in Lunigiana. These sheep have a a distinctive, almost prehistoric look, and their meat is of excellent quality and unique in taste. I cook Zeri lamb for special occasions, it's so good.

Although Cinzia had given me directions to the mountain where she keeps her herd, she didn't tell me how difficult it would be to get there. Cinzia and her herd live on the very top of the mountains, and the road seemed to go almost straight up at times. My good old Range Rover moaned as she took the winding switchbacks up, up, and up.

Cinzia met me near the top, driving an ancient Fiat Panda, with her half-wolf, half-German shepherd in the front seat beside her. She released the passenger side door, and the wolf-dog took the lead of the Italian shepherding dogs, called Maremmas, up the path. Once we reached the top I commented to Cinzia on how dangerous the drive is. She looked at me blankly and said, "Let's go, and watch out for wolves." I misunderstood her and thought she was referring to her wolf-dog, so I asked again in Italian, "Be careful of your wolf-dog?" "No," she repeated, "beware of the wolves." Now I was really scared, and I realized that caring for a flock is no joke. We walked up the path for a minute, and Cinzia stopped and said, "Wait here!"

At this point I was a little afraid to be on my own, but there were dogs around, and it is said a Maremma is a match for a wolf. All of a sudden I heard the clanging of a hundred bells, as the Zeri sheep were being herded to the pasture below to graze. I jumped out of the way of their frenzied run and got a first good look at them. I read somewhere that a large flock of sheep is referred to as a "mob," and I now know why.

I followed the sheep and the dogs, keeping close to Cinzia as she minded her herd. Cinzia is a no-nonsense, hard-working woman who says very little and only when asked a question. I understand that being a shepherdess is a solitary and hard life. Doing this ancient work must be a passion, a calling—and Cinzia obviously has it. She loves her flock, her dogs, and the land.

We waved goodbye without saying a word.

ROASTED HERBED LAMB SHOULDER
with Potatoes
(AGNELLO DI ZERI CON PATATE)

This recipe comes from a lovely shepherdess in Zeri, who prepared it for us one magical, bucolic afternoon. Zeri is a lovely hamlet known for its delicious lamb, located in the heart of Lunigiana. The lambs, raised free-range and organically, leisurely graze on sweet grass all day in the beautiful countryside. This is an ancient shepherd's recipe, a one-pot meat-and-potato stew cooked over a fire in the fields—and it's still cooked that way to this day. Although this recipe is heavy on herbs, it doesn't include garlic or onion, which is typical of dishes from northern Italy. You will never miss them, though, because of the depth of flavors the herbs offer. The shepherds would carry dried herbs in their pack to use when they cooked in the fields. In this recipe I use both dried and fresh for roasting.

Serves 4 to 6

4 pounds lamb shoulder chops or lamb chops

1 teaspoon dried sage

1 teaspoon dried rosemary

1 teaspoon dried thyme

1 teaspoon dried marjoram

1 teaspoon salt

1 pound fingerling potatoes, washed and dried

⅓ cup extra virgin olive oil

1 cup white wine

3 sprigs fresh sage

3 sprigs fresh rosemary

3 sprigs fresh thyme

Preheat the oven to 375°F.

Place the lamb shoulder chops in a large Dutch oven.

In a bowl combine the sage, rosemary, thyme, marjoram, and salt, and sprinkle the herb mixture over both sides of the lamb shoulder pieces. Tuck the potatoes around the lamb. Top with the oil and wine. Tuck in the fresh sage, rosemary, and thyme sprigs, cover, and roast for 1 hour. Do not lift the cover of the Dutch oven while roasting—this is very important. Once you lift the cover, the lamb and potatoes should be nicely browned. Serve warm right from the pot, as they do in the fields.

PORK SCALLOPINI
with Creamy Porcini Mushroom Sauce
(SCALLOPINE DI MAIALE AI PORCINI)

Pork scallopini is a traditional dish in this region and locals use many different sauces with it. I don't think of scallopini as a country recipe—I often see it on sophisticated menus—but it truly is. The dried porcinis have an intensified, earthy, smoky flavor, and I actually prefer them to fresh porcinis in my sauces and soups.

Serves 4 to 6

1 cup dried porcini mushrooms

6 thin boneless pork chops (3 pounds)

1 cup all-purpose flour

1 teaspoon salt

½ teaspoon freshly ground black pepper

¼ cup plus 3 tablespoons extra virgin olive oil, divided, plus more as needed

1 clove garlic, minced

3 tablespoons unsalted butter

2 small shallots, chopped

1 cup white wine

3 tablespoons fresh thyme

¾ cup heavy cream

Juice of ½ lemon

⅓ cup chopped fresh flat-leaf parsley

Preheat the oven to 200°F.

Soak the whole, dried mushrooms in 1 cup of warm water for 1 hour to soften, then drain the mushrooms, set aside in a bowl, and discard the soaking liquid.

Place the pork chops between 2 pieces of plastic wrap and use a mallet to lightly pound to ½ inch thick.

In a shallow bowl, mix the flour, salt, and pepper, then dredge each chop in the flour mixture. Shake off any excess flour.

Add ¼ cup oil to a frying pan over medium heat, and brown the pork chops three at a time for 3 to 5 minutes on each side. Repeat the process for the second batch, adding extra oil if needed. Drain on paper towels and place on a pan in the oven to keep warm.

To prepare the mushroom sauce, add the remaining 3 tablespoons oil to a frying pan over medium heat and sauté the mushrooms and garlic for 5 minutes. Add the butter and shallots, stir to combine, and sauté for 2 minutes. Stir in the wine and thyme and simmer for 5 minutes. Reduce the heat to low and stir in the cream; simmer until the sauce thickens slightly.

Transfer the scallopini to a platter and top with the mushroom sauce, drizzle with lemon juice, and garnish with parsley.

CHESTNUT CAKE
with Nuts
(CASTAGNACCIO)

This is a thin, dense freeform cake traditionally baked in parchment, or on a sheet pan, then cut into squares (think thin brownies). The raisins add a touch of sweetness. It's topped with walnuts and pine nuts, and is popular eaten with a cup of tea or a glass of red wine. Or add a dollop of fresh ricotta and serve as dessert with vin santo.

Serves 6 to 8

½ cup raisins

1 ½ cups chestnut flour, sifted

3 tablespoons extra virgin olive oil, divided

Pinch fine sea salt

⅓ cup toasted walnuts, roughly chopped

⅓ cup pine nuts

1 tablespoon fresh rosemary

Preheat the oven to 350°F. Soak the raisins in warm water to cover for 10 to 15 minutes until plumped and soft. Drain well, and squeeze them gently in a cloth to get rid of any excess water.

Place the chestnut flour in a large bowl, and gradually whisk in 2 cups warm water to form a thick, smooth batter. Whisk in 2 tablespoons olive oil, the salt, and raisins. Mix well with a wooden spoon.

Pour onto a sheet pan lined with parchment paper. Sprinkle the top with the walnuts, pine nuts, and rosemary, and drizzle with the remaining tablespoon of olive oil. Pat lightly with a spatula to adhere to the parchment, and bake for about 30 to 35 minutes, or until firm and lightly browned. When cooled, cut into squares and serve at room temperature.

Chef and Artisanal Winemaker, Restaurant Proprietors, and Modern Farmers, Sara and Francesca Aliboni

Meet Sara and Francesca, the wildly talented sisters and proprietors of a beautiful, sustainable restaurant and winery named Cà Vidè, located high on a hilltop in Caprognano, a small village founded in 1649 by a man named Signore Marchini, near the city of Fosdinovo.

The drive to the village is on a narrow road that winds high up into the mountains, with breathtaking views along precarious curves—it's an exciting journey. The village seems to hang off the mountainside. When I saw it three years ago, I thought it was a bucolic wonderland! All the ancient houses have been lovingly restored.

Francesca and Sara's family have lived in the village for more than a hundred years. Their parents were the first to begin renovations, and as Francesca and Sara had families of their own, over time they completed the restoration of all of the village houses, the restaurant, and a small farm. The village is completely occupied by their family, their parents, aunts and uncles, cousins, and a few close friends. All the children grow up together—idyllic, if you ask me.

On that first visit, I was greeted by Francesca, the energetic young vintner. The family was in the midst of refurbishing the last part of the village, a beloved chapel built in the late seventeenth century by Signore Marchini, and as we walked toward her restaurant on the stone path, she explained how they would return the chapel to its former glory. The village itself, with cats and kids running happily all around the town center, seemed right out of a fairy tale—I expected to see the Pied Piper around any corner.

At the restaurant, Francesca is the winemaker and works the front of house; her sister, Sara, is the restaurant's chef. She told me that her entire family lived in the village and worked the vineyards and on their farm. "Even the children help pick grapes and produce," she said. She went on to explain that their goal was to live a fully self-sustained life. "Everything is upcycled or composted," she said, pointing to the sky, "and the power is from the sun." All the habitants of this utopia abide by the same code, "Nothing is wasted." I was smitten with the concept.

Their family and friends refurbished the small farm on four acres. They revived the vineyard and planted acres of vegetables and fruit trees. Cà Vidè, the name of their restaurant, means Vidè's House, named for their grandmother, the matriarch. All the products they use in the restaurant are sourced from their garden. The delicious menu is seasonal and very creative, featuring traditional dishes with a modern twist. All the wine comes from their vineyard, and the oil is from their olive trees. It is a truly authentic and local experience. Their respect for the land and the earth bonded us immediately. All their dishes are memorable, but the one thing I would drive for miles to get is their corn focaccia. It's chewy, crunchy, salty, and oily, with a texture I had never tasted before. When I asked them for the recipe for this book, I expected a no, but to my surprise and gratitude they graciously agreed.

CÀ VIDÈ FOCACCIA

This focaccia calls for several different and unusual flours—including the wonderful 7-grain flour from the Moro mill (see Source Guide, page 205) and finely ground corn flour—that give it a chewy bite and delicious flavor. The whole grains also make it healthier than traditional focaccia. Bakers will note this is a firmer dough than most focaccias—it tastes like an earthy flatbread. I like to use brick yeast during times I plan to make a lot of bread, because the shelf life is not as long as that of dry yeast, or packaged yeast. The compressed version is fresh yeast that is 70 percent moisture, and is used by most professional bakers. It has a slightly stronger taste. You first "bloom" it in water just to ensure the yeast is activated. Note: This recipe only proofs once; whereas most focaccia goes through a second rise, this one does not.

Makes one (13 x 18-inch) loaf

1 teaspoon crumbled brick yeast, available at most groceries

1 ½ cups 00 flour, plus 2 tablespoons, for kneading

3 tablespoons bread or all-purpose flour

1 cup 7-grain flour (see Source Guide, page 205)

¾ cup corn flour, plus more for rolling

1 tablespoon salt

3 tablespoons extra virgin olive oil, plus ¼ cup for baking

In a small bowl, whisk the yeast into 1 cup warm water and set aside for 10 minutes until bubbles form.

In a large bowl, combine 1 ½ cups 00 flour, the bread flour, the 7-grain flour, and ¾ cup corn flour and salt. Add the yeast mixture and 3 tablespoons olive oil, and mix for about 1 minute until it forms a shaggy dough ball that holds together.

Transfer the dough to a work surface lightly floured with 00 flour and knead for about 5 minutes, until it forms a sturdy ball—it will be firmer than a traditional focaccia dough. Test by pressing the dough with your fingers; it should bounce back. Return it to the large bowl, cover with a towel or plastic wrap, and place it in a warm spot for 2 hours to proof. The dough should double in size.

Preheat the oven to 400°F.

Dust a clean board or work surface with a little corn flour. Transfer the proofed dough to the board and roll out to a 13 by 18-inch rectangle, about ¼ inch thick.

Coat a 13 by 18-inch baking sheet with 1 tablespoon olive oil. Use your fingers to stretch the rolled dough to fit the baking sheet, all the way into the corners. Drizzle with the remaining 3 tablespoons olive oil and 3 tablespoons water. Rub the oil and water over the top of the focaccia then dimple the surface using your fingers.

Bake for about 20 to 25 minutes, until golden brown. Let cool slightly, then cut into pieces and serve warm. Although it does hold up well the next day, this focaccia is best served fresh.

Note: At La Fortezza I divide the dough in half, roll both halves out to only ⅛ inch thick, and bake for 20 to 25 minutes in 2 batches to make crackers. They are delicious to serve with cheese and spreads!

MAROCCA DI CASOLA
(CHESTNUT BREAD)

Marocca di Casola is a dense, spongy bread that you'll want on your charcuterie board. It teams up perfectly with ricotta, honey, anchovies, and lardo di Colonnata or pancetta. This bread is listed as an official Slow Food product for this region of Italy. Pane marocca is an ancient bread, at least 350 years old. Thanks to local artisanal baker Fabrizio Bertolucci, the tradition is alive and well. His passion and talent for making it and selling it throughout Italy has made him well known, and he generously shares his recipe here with us. Serve with lardo, or fresh ricotta drizzled with honey; it's also great with prosciutto and jam.

The finely ground wheat flour, used in addition to the chestnut flour, absorbs liquid faster than coarser grains, so it's used often for baked goods and pastries. ✄ *Makes two 6-inch diameter loaves*

---

8 ounces russet potatoes (2 small), peeled

2 teaspoons salt

1 tablespoon plus 1 teaspoon extra virgin olive oil

⅔ cup chestnut flour

4 cups finely ground wheat flour, available at specialty grocers

1 cup sourdough starter (recipe, page 189)

1 teaspoon brewer's yeast (see Source Guide, page 205)

Fill a pot with enough water to cover the potatoes and bring to a boil over medium-high heat. Cook 10 to 12 minutes, until tender, then drain and let cool. Transfer to a large mixing bowl, mash them with a fork, and season with the salt and olive oil.

In a separate large bowl, combine both flours, the sourdough starter, and ⅓ cup water. Set the mixture aside at room temperature to rise, at least 4 hours. (Note: It does not rise much; it will gain about 25 percent in volume.) After the flours have proofed, add the potatoes to the dough, knead until roughly combined, transfer to a flour-dusted board, and sprinkle the brewer's yeast on the dough.

Alternatively, you can place the dough into the bowl of a standing mixer fitted with a dough hook, sprinkle the brewer's yeast into the bowl and knead until combined, about 5 minutes. Form the dough into two 6-inch diameter round loaves and let them rise for 40 to 60 minutes. Note: Again, it does not rise much; it will only gain a little volume.

Preheat the oven to 450°F.

Cut an inch-deep slash or cross on the top of both loaves with a sharp blade and bake on a stone or a baking sheet for 35 to 40 minutes, until the bread is dark brown and sounds hollow when tapped on the bottom.

A Word About Chestnut Flour

Chestnut flour is a staple ingredient in Lungiana. In autumn, chestnuts are collected and dried for forty days in a little hut in the woods known as a *metato*, where the fire is fed with chestnut wood. Once dried, they are gradually ground into flour by millstones. The best time to buy the chestnut flour is end of November to early December, when the new flour is finally available at market.

The old mill Rossi in Fivizzano dates back to 1898, and today it is still considered the best at milling cereals and chestnuts, using a heavy, traditional millstone.

Chestnut flour is the key ingredient of traditional recipes from Lunigiana, including Tuscan chestnut gnocchi boiled in milk; castagnaccio (recipe, page 185), a type of chestnut cake; and marocca.

SOURDOUGH STARTER (PASTA MADRE)

Breadmaking traditions in Italy commonly begin with a sourdough starter called pasta madre, *or* lievito madre. *Typically, the madre is fed with flour daily, or twice daily, but maintenance varies according to each baker's practices. Feeding once every 12 hours will increase the rate at which the sourdough starter can multiply; feeding every 24 hours will mean the starter takes a bit longer, but may be more sustainable, depending on your time commitment.*

Yields 1 cup starter

¾ cup all-purpose flour
½ cup warm water (80 to 85°F)

Combine the flour and water in a large glass or plastic container (at least 2 quarts; you want to give it room to grow). Stir vigorously to incorporate air, and cover with a cheesecloth.

Leave in a warm place (70 to 85°F) for 12 to 24 hours, depending on how often you want to feed it. At the 12- or 24-hour mark, you may begin to see some bubbles, indicating that organisms are present. Repeat the feeding with another ½ cup warm

water and ¾ cup flour. Stir vigorously, cover, and wait another 12 to 24 hours.

After the third feeding you must remove and discard half the starter before every future feeding.

After about 5 to 7 days the sourdough starter should have enough yeast and bacteria to be used for baking. It can then be covered and stored in the refrigerator. If fed every day, this starter will keep for years.

Bread Baker, Fabio Bertolucci

As in all stories of cucina povera, la Marocca di Casola is an ancient type of bread typical of one small rural area (Casola, Lunigiana) in northern Italy. Lunigiana is filled with chestnut trees, and in ancient times bread makers discovered that the slow-roasted and dried chestnuts could be turned into useful and nutritional flour for making bread. The story goes that the inhabitants sold olives and olive oil to earn a living, and came up with innovative ways to utilize the chestnuts to feed themselves. Many

houses still have roasting/drying sheds. La Fortezza's drying room was at the top of the tower, where our master bedroom is now located. The entire top floor was blackened from the soot when I first saw it. In ancient times, all houses had low-burning fires in the drying rooms, used for heat and cooking, as well as for drying the chestnuts to use as flour.

I met Fabio six years ago at a local market in Fivizzano. I was fascinated to learn that he had decided to revitalize the art of ancient breadmaking. A while later, I started putting together slow food experiences at La Fortezza, and I remembered him and asked if I could visit his bakery. Of course, he agreed and our friendship began.

Fabio's lovely little bakery is in a tiny village high in the mountains. He makes about one hundred loaves every other day, and distributes them to local groceries, bakeries, and restaurants. His kitchen in the back of the building is humble—the industrial mixer takes up half the space. The front of the bakery houses the wood-burning oven, the forno. The bread is made by mixing finely sieved chestnut flour (which gives the bread its dense, characteristic flavor) with wheat flour, boiled and mashed potatoes, extra virgin olive oil, yeast, a sourdough starter, and water. The dough is formed into a round loaf, about 8 inches in diameter, and is left to rise for more than an hour before being baked in the wood-burning oven.

Fabio pulls every loaf of marocca bread from the oven himself. His is a solitary existence and a life with purpose and exquisite simplicity—he prefers to work alone. I often tease him that he's like a monk, which makes him laugh. Fabio's mission is to reintroduce this bread to Italy and the world. He always hands me a hot loaf wrapped in a brown paper bag when I leave. It is the best gift, and I take it gratefully in anticipation of sinking my teeth into a warm slice, slathered with local butter and chestnut honey from the beehives down the road. Marocca bread has recently been recognized as a protected traditional local bread by a Slow Food Presidium. Although hard to find in other markets, it's slowly making its mark at Slow Food festivals outside the region.

CHESTNUT PANCAKES
(NECCI)

These soft, thin pancakes have a hint of a chocolaty, nutty flavor—lovely as breakfast or dessert, or rolled up with ricotta cream, Nutella, or your favorite jam. I also love using Giovanna's Grape Jam (recipe, page 151).

Makes 4 to 8 pancakes

2 ½ cups chestnut flour, sifted

½ cup all-purpose flour

1 teaspoon sugar

½ teaspoon salt

½ teaspoon baking power

4 cups sparkling water

About 3 tablespoons extra virgin olive oil

For the ricotta cream:

1 cup ricotta

1 teaspoon grated lemon zest

3 tablespoons fresh lemon juice

1 tablespoon sugar

In a large bowl, whisk together both flours, sugar, salt, baking powder, and sparkling water until the mixture forms a smooth and very loose dough. Cover and set aside at room temperature for at least 1 hour, or overnight in the refrigerator—just make sure to bring it to room temperature before making the pancakes.

When you are ready to cook, heat a small nonstick sauté pan over medium heat and add about 1 teaspoon oil. Pour a scant ¼ cup batter into the pan. Tilt the pan and rotate so that the batter runs to the edges, creating a thin, even layer. Immediately loosen the edges with a spatula and cook for 1 minute, or until the top is set and looks dry. Flip, and cook for 15 to 30 seconds. Transfer to an individual serving plate.

Add a little more oil to the pan before pouring the next ¼ cup batter. Repeat with all the remaining oil and batter.

To prepare the ricotta cream: Stir together the ricotta, lemon zest, lemon juice, and sugar until smooth.

Spread each pancake with the ricotta cream, and roll up. Serve warm.

HOLIDAY NUT PIE OF PONTREMOLI (LA SPONGATA DI PONTREMOLI)

The spongata di Pontremoli is a fruit and nut pie from the medieval town of Pontremoli, in the heart of Lunigiana, and it has Jewish origins, first appearing in the sixteenth century. History says Sephardic Jews fleeing the Spanish Inquisition brought it to Italy. The main component, a paste of dried and candied fruit, is similar to charoseth, *a fruit compote traditionally served during Passover. The spongata has a delicious honey-soaked, fruitcake-like quality to it; and it's served during both Jewish and Christian holidays.*

✵ *Serves 8 to 10*

....

For the pastry:

2 cups all-purpose flour, plus more for work surface

¾ cup confectioners' sugar

¼ teaspoon salt

1 stick plus 3 tablespoons unsalted butter, cut into small cubes, at room temperature

1 egg yolk

¼ cup white wine, plus more as needed

Zest of 1 lemon, grated

¼ cup plus 1 tablespoon fig jam

For the filling:

¼ cup blanched almonds, roughly chopped

¼ cup blanched hazelnuts, roughly chopped

2 tablespoons pine nuts

½ cup dried figs, chopped

½ cup chopped candied orange peel (recipe, page 194)

¼ cup raisins

¼ teaspoon ground cinnamon

½ teaspoon ground cloves

¼ teaspoon freshly grated nutmeg

½ cup honey

¼ teaspoon salt

For finishing:

1 egg yolk beaten with 2 tablespoons water, for egg wash

1 tablespoon granulated sugar, for sprinkling the top

....

Preheat the oven to 350°F.

To prepare the pastry: In the bowl of a standing mixer fitted with the paddle attachment, combine 2 cups flour, confectioners' sugar, salt, and butter. Blend on medium speed for about 3 to 5 minutes until the dough resembles crumbs. Add the egg yolk, ¼ cup wine, and lemon zest and mix until a soft ball forms.

Transfer the dough to a lightly floured work surface, then roll into a ball and divide the dough in half. Form into 2 disks, wrap both in plastic wrap, and refrigerate for at least 1 hour, or up to 1 day.

Remove the dough from the refrigerator and let it rest at room temperature for 30 minutes before rolling. On a lightly floured work surface, roll out both disks to 10-inch-diameter rounds about ¼ inch thick.

Fit a parchment paper round into a 9½-inch fluted tart pan with a removable bottom, then set 1 pastry round into the pan on top of the parchment. Spread the fig jam over the pastry.

To make the filling: combine all the filling ingredients in a bowl and mix well. Spread the filling on top of the fig jam.

Cover with the remaining pastry round, seal and trim around the edges, and use your fingers to create a fluted pattern around the circumference of the pie. Decorate the top if desired. Brush the top with the egg wash and sprinkle with the granulated sugar. Bake for about 30 minutes, until the edges are golden brown and the surface is shiny and cracked. Cool and serve.

CANDIED ORANGE PEEL

✤ *Makes about 1 cup*

1 large orange, ¼ inch sliced off the top and bottom

5 tablespoons sugar, divided

Cut the peel on the orange into 4 vertical segments. Remove each segment (including white pith) in 1 piece. Cut into ½-inch-wide strips.

Bring 3 tablespoons sugar and 1 cup water to a boil in a medium saucepan over medium heat, stirring to dissolve the sugar. Add the peel and return to a boil; then reduce the heat to low and simmer for 30 minutes, stirring often, until the peel is very soft. Make sure to stir and watch closely so as not to burn the peel.

Drain the peel, place on a rack on a baking sheet to dry, and sprinkle with the remaining 2 tablespoons sugar. Make sure to separate the strips; you can use 2 forks to do this. Leave to dry for 1 day, until the peels are dry to the touch. At this point, you can enjoy the candied peel immediately, or place in a zip-tight bag and freeze it for up to 2 months.

GIOVANNA'S CHESTNUT JAM

The chestnut looks like a porcupine or sea urchin when it falls on the ground. You have to split the spiky shell open to get to the round, smooth brown chestnut inside. Chestnuts have a distinctive alkaline mouthfeel, with a soft, nutty flavor. In this recipe, the rum rounds out the nutty flavor. Consider this jam the country sister of almond or hazelnut butter. You can order chestnuts from farmers in the fall, or online year-round (see Source Guide, page 205). If using fresh chestnuts, roast them for 20 minutes in a 325°F oven for additional smoky flavor. Giovanna likes her chestnut jam a little chunky, but I prefer mine smooth and spreadable. ✄ **Makes four 10-ounce jars**

4 cups peeled chestnuts (about 1 ½ pounds)

1 cup sugar

2 teaspoons vanilla extract

1 teaspoon salt

½ cup rum (optional)

In a large bowl, cover the chestnuts with lukewarm water, and let soak for 2 hours at room temperature until softened, then drain.

In a heavy pot, combine the chestnuts, sugar, vanilla, salt, 3 cups water, and the rum (if using) over low heat. Bring to a simmer and cook for 2 to 3 hours, until the chestnuts are nearly falling apart. The water will evaporate, so keep a close eye on the pot and add more water as needed.

Place the chestnuts along with their cooking liquid into a food processor fitted with a metal blade, and pulse to your desired texture.

Fill a large pot one-third full of water and heat on the stovetop until a thermometer reads 180°F. Check the jars, lids, and bands for proper functioning, and place them in the hot water for 10 minutes to sterilize. Use a jar lifter to remove each preheated jar and drain them on a clean cloth towel. Fill the jars with the jam to ½ inch from the top, and tighten the lids.

These will keep in the refrigerator for up to 6 months.

Moro Olive Mill and Flour Mill Proprietors, Monica and Adriano Moro

I was first introduced to the Moro family by a local chef, and thrilled to meet the owners of this small, yet productive, olive mill. Much to my delight, I soon discovered that not only did they mill the finest olive oil, but they also ran a flour mill. It's the perfect one-stop shop!

The Moros grows their own wheat and corn, and they mill nuts from local groves all over Lunigiana. Theirs are delicious, high-quality flours that I enjoy baking with, and most of the area's chefs are regular customers as well. The mill offer a big selection of flours—I love the 7-grain flour, which is used in Cà Vidè Focaccia (recipe, page 187), 0 flour (all-purpose flour), and 00 flour, which is great for pizza crusts. They also have a specific pasta flour that falls somewhere between the 0 and 00; a rustic whole wheat and semolina flour; and corn flours, both coarse and finely ground. They also offer chickpea, oat, almond, chestnut, potato, hazelnut, rice, and coconut flours.

The mill, started by Alfredo Moro in 1954, produces its own products, and operates in autumn as a press for the local all-organic growers. The parking lot starts filling up with trucks laden with olives in October, and is jam-packed with growers until January.

The family business is overseen by a brother and sister team, Monica and Adriano, who run the day-to-day operation. Their parents are still very active in the business, and on any given day Mamma will offer you a great recipe as you pay for your goods. Papà is regularly spotted driving a tractor to the groves. Sometimes you can see their grandchildren in the parking lot, chasing the family dog.

I wait for their fresh pressed olive oil every October. Their flours are exclusively used in all our pastas, pizza, bread doughs, and tart crusts at La Fortezza.

CHOCOLATE CHESTNUT-FLOUR BUNDT CAKE
(CIAMBELLONE CON FARINA DI CASTAGNE)

I serve this dense, flavorful cake with ice cream or fruit, or doused with a liqueur like marsala or vin santo. Because of the chestnut flour, the cake is as moist on day four as on day one. If you're a chocaholic like me, feel free to double the amount of chocolate chips—I have. ✖ *Serves 8 to 10*

4 large eggs

1 ½ cups packed light brown sugar

1 teaspoon vanilla extract

½ cup milk

½ cup (1 stick) melted unsalted butter, plus 1 teaspoon for buttering the pan

1 cup all-purpose flour, plus 1 teaspoon for flouring the pan

1 ½ cups chestnut flour

1 teaspoon ground cinnamon

1 teaspoon baking powder

½ teaspoon salt

1 to 2 cups semisweet chocolate chips (see headnote)

Confectioners' sugar, for finishing

Preheat the oven to 350°F.

In the bowl of a standing mixer fitted with a paddle attachment, combine the eggs and sugar and mix on medium speed until fluffy, about 5 minutes. Add the vanilla, milk, and melted butter and blend for about 2 to 3 minutes until smooth.

In a separate bowl, whisk together both flours, the cinnamon, baking powder, and salt. Add to the egg mixture and beat on medium speed until smooth. By hand, stir in the chocolate chips.

Pour the batter into a greased and floured 10-cup Bundt pan and bake for 45 to 55 minutes, until a toothpick placed in the center comes out clean.

Let cool completely, then remove from the pan and sprinkle with confectioners' sugar.

INDEX

Page numbers in italics indicate illustrations

SOURCE GUIDE

Alma Gourmet: almagourmet.com/store
Chanterelles
Chestnut flour
Chickpea flour
Dried porcini mushrooms
Farro
Fresh porcini mushrooms
Lardo
Pecorino
Pine nuts
Truffles
Wild fennel seeds
Wild fennel pollen

Amazon: amazon.com
Brewer's yeast
Caputo Cuor di Cereali multigrain flour
Chestnuts, boiled and peeled
Dried Sicilian capers

Eataly: eataly.com/us_en/shop
Balsamic vinegar
Chestnut honey
Fresh truffles
Mutti Polpa tomatoes
Parmesan cheese

Gourmet Italian: gourmetitalian.com
00 flour

Gustiamo: gustiamo.com
Bottarga
Capers in salt

Northfork Bison: northforkbison.com
Wild boar

Oilala: oilala.com
Tuna-stuffed peppers

Tartufi Ponzio: tartufiponzio.com
Fresh truffles

Teitel Brothers: teitelbros.com
Pecorino ricotta salata

Purveyors:

Agriturismo Podere Conti: podereconti.com

Fabio Bertolucci: instagram.com/lamaroccadi casola

Nadia Bongi: instagram.com/az.agr_bongi_antonio

Cà Vidè: facebook.com/AgriturismoCaVide

Simone Mori: truffleexcursion.com

Frantoio Moro: oliomoro.it/en

Paolo Varella: instagram.com/paolo_varrella

Giovanna Zurlo: agriturismodiladallacqua.it

Slow Food: slowfood.com

UNESCO: unesco.it/it/RiserveBiosfera/Detail/93

ACKNOWLEDGMENTS

La Fortezza, and this cookbook, would not be the same without the amazing people who live and work around me. I am eternally grateful to all the beautiful, rugged, brilliant people who came into my life after we made the leap and renovated this ancient fortress in the middle of the Tuscan countryside. Everyone opened their hearts and accepted us, no questions asked—just the one: How can we help? *Grazie mille* to Giovanna, for introducing me to everything food-related, becoming a regular in our kitchen, and teaching me to cook the local fare. Federica is kind, talented, and always supportive—plus, I love her family's amaro. Hats off to our groundskeeper and head gardener, Gianluca, for planting and tending our garden; his wisdom and kindness are unparalleled. To Cornelia, a true friend and advisor, you have helped me more than you know. Barbara has shown me that even later in life you can meet your best friend and soul sister—thank you for your wisdom, your kind friendship, and for your great taste. I'm so happy you prop-styled this book with me. Thank you to my amazing La Fortezza team for all you do to help promote and share this beautiful vision. Of course I could not go without a heartfelt thank you to my amazing photographer, David Loftus. David's beautiful images reflect the true beauty here in Lunigiana on every page. He's truly a gentleman and a scholar, and an incredible artist. I feel honored to have him be a big part of this book and humbled to call him a friend. David also introduced me to the fabulous food stylist Rosie Scott and I am forever grateful because she brought so much beauty to the recipes. Of course, thank you to local chef Leo Ceri—I could not have done this book without you. I want to thank my book packager Janice Shay; she truly gets me and gets the immense love I have for this region. She is always insightful, honest, passionate, and, most important, a delight to work with. This is our fourth book together and I cannot think of anyone else that I would rather create and write with. Janice, you know I love you, a million thanks.

A cookbook never gets published without lots of testing and tasting and discussion of recipes and dishes. There were a lot of conversations, texts, and emails early in the morning and late at night, comparing ratios for the Italian recipes I was presented by various purveyors in the book—many that had little or no measurements, and sometimes with key ingredients missing—which facilitated comparing notes, analyzing the recipe, then tweaking amounts and techniques to fit the American kitchen. It may have been my favorite part of the process. So, I want to thank the La Fortezza cookbook testing team: Oma Blaise Ford, Marc Pollack, and Steve Mckenzie. They're an amazing group of fantastic cooks who patiently tested and tasted, then commented on the recipes. I could not have done it without you all. Here's to cooking, eating, drinking, and making beautiful memories together in the Italian countryside!